Project Technology

CONTROL
TECHNOLOGY
teachers' handbook

Hodder and Stoughton Educational

First published 1975 for the Schools Council
by English Universities Press Ltd
now Hodder and Stoughton Educational
a division of Hodder and Stoughton Ltd
Mill Road, Dunton Green, Sevenoaks, Kent
Reprinted 1975 (twice), 1976, 1977, 1978, 1980, 1982

ISBN   0 340 18243 1

Printed in Great Britain by
Biddles Ltd., Guildford, Surrey.

Contents

Foreword

Project Technology was a major curriculum development project initiated by the Schools Council to promote a better understanding by boys and girls in school of the importance and relevance of technology. The Project was concerned with helping teachers to stimulate an awareness of the material and scientific forces which effect change in our society and to develop knowledge of these forces and their means of control by the direct involvement of pupils in technological activities.

The Project Technology teaching-material programme is the result of a careful assessment of what is required in the schools, followed by trials and editing of the material itself. The Project Technology team felt that it was essential to draw on the experience, imagination and flair of individual teachers who, over a period of years, had developed technological work in particular parts of the school curriculum.

It is against this background that the Control Technology course should be seen. Other teaching material, notably the Project Technology Handbooks series, indicates both a thematic and a tactical approach to school technology. All of this reflects the diverse nature of the work being done and of the alternative teaching methods and organisation which are possible.

This course, however, is intended to meet the needs of those schools who wish to develop a structured and sequential two- or three-year course, covering an important area of technology. Some teachers have expressed the view that, while appreciating the value of what might be regarded as the more fortuitous involvement of pupils with technological projects and investigations, they should welcome a more systemic course approach.

The joint authors of Control Technology, Messrs G.J. Fox and D.F. Marshall, have developed the course over a number of years at Danum Grammar School for Boys, Doncaster, where they were given essential support and encouragement by the Headmaster (Mr E. Semper, OBE) and by the Doncaster Education Authority.

Clearly defined educational objectives were established, and the appropriate teaching methods, based on pupil assignments, with appropriate texts and equipment, were progressively developed, with the support of the Project Technology team.

First-stage school trials were conducted in selected schools in the Doncaster area with the generous help of the LEA. Secondary trials followed in various parts of the country. We are especially grateful to the teachers in these schools for the help and co-operation they provided for the authors, the Project Technology team (led by Mr G.L. Viles) and the Evaluators appointed by the Schools Council.

The Control Technology course has been carefully based on purpose-built equipment essential to the effective running of the course. A considerable effort has been put into the development of this equipment, at all stages, and we are indebted to all concerned, including the present suppliers. More recently, Trent Polytechnic are to be thanked for encouraging further development work by the National Centre for School Technology.

General introduction to the course

THE NEED FOR NEW COURSES

The Control Technology course is part of the teaching material
produced by Project Technology to enable teachers to stimulate an
awareness of the material and scientific forces which effect change
in our society. The course also enables pupils to experience the
purposeful application of knowledge in an increasingly significant
area of technology, affecting the working and domestic life of more
and more people.

Work of a technological character is attempted in some schools
through existing science and craft courses, but the work undertaken
is often limited by syllabus requirements, especially in examined
courses. An approach that will stimulate a greater awareness of
the modern technological environment is needed. It must excite the
imagination of children, including the applied scientists and
engineers of the future. Although young children are naturally
imaginative and inventive, the teacher's experience often confirms
that this innate curiosity diminishes rapidly beyond the age of
about 13 years. Many attempts to bring technological project work
into the curriculum result in only modest success, since progress
is often slow and can lead to frustration unless the student meets
with frequent success. Too often success is achieved only after
considerable time has been spent on constructional work or when the
teacher has 'rescued' the project by giving excessive guidance and
encouragement.

New courses for 13 year olds are, therefore, needed which will:

1 maintain and stimulate the inventiveness of pupils;

2 enable construction time to be kept to a minimum, thus giving
   confidence and encouraging experimentation with alternative
   solutions;

3 provide stimulating problems which will motivate children and
   require the minimum teacher contribution;

4 provide a rich variety of background information and techniques,
   enabling a number of solutions to be formulated to a given
   problem;

5 provide training and a logical approach to project work which
   will be especially valuable to the potential sixth-former;

6   be complementary to existing craft and science courses by
    emphasising the applications of scientific principles;

7   be flexible enough to keep pace with developments in technology;

8   allow children to work at their own pace, and also extend the
    brighter ones;

9   enable teachers without specialist qualifications to become
    involved.

THE CONTROL TECHNOLOGY COURSE

The course in Control Technology attempts to satisfy the above
requirements. It was designed, in the first instance, for average
and above average boys who might, or might not, be taking O-level
or CSE courses in physics, metalwork, or woodwork. Some schools
have used the course with mixed groups of boys and girls.

OUTLINE OF THE COURSE

The course is intended to last for three years, on the basis of two
forty-minute periods per week in the third form and four periods
per week in the fourth and fifth forms. A series of carefully
programmed investigations and experiments, using purpose-designed
equipment, should take approximately half the total time allocation.
They are designed to cover the relevant subject matter and to
provide experience in the solution of problems. The remainder of
the time is to be used for projects of varying lengths. It will be
appreciated that in the earlier stages of the course all of the
time is given up to the programmed sequence of units and suggested
mini-projects. Where necessary, important concepts are developed
further by teacher demonstrations and discussions. The specially
designed, easy-to-use, reliable equipment ensures rapid progress.
In the latter stages of the course the bulk of the time is given up
to longer and more open-ended projects.

Some schools have successfully conducted the course on a two-year
basis, but this inevitably means that less time is available for
the major projects during the final year.

EDUCATIONAL OBJECTIVES

1   To provide sufficient background knowledge to enable pupils to
    solve complex problems involving the making, control, and auto-
    mation of devices.

2

2　To encourage them to think creatively and to produce original, imaginative work.

3　To promote the ability to analyse what is involved in a new situation.

4　To promote the ability to select and apply principles, methods, and procedures, and to conceive probable solutions.

5　To promote the ability to synthesise and, thereafter, to plan and possibly to construct a device.

6　To promote the ability to recognise the limitations of a design, and to modify or suggest modifications to it.

7　To give pupils confidence in using unfamiliar and possibly complex equipment.

8　To encourage pupils to record their work in a clear fashion, including successes and failures.

PROGRAMMED NOTES

Each programmed unit consists of:

1　pupils' assignments

2　pupils' follow-up sheets, which:

  a) provide possible solutions and relevant information,
  b) confirm the fundamental principles involved,
  c) prepare the ground for the next assignment,
  d) give background information.

The units are designed:

1　to allow pupils to work at their own pace, to extend their background knowledge, and to ensure that adequate information is given at the right time;

2　to enable teachers to give help to individuals or groups in difficulty;

3　to assist teachers who have limited specialist knowledge.

In addition, the extensive Teachers' Notes provide:

  1　details of special demonstrations;
  2　constructional details of special equipment;
  3　sources of supply of material;

4   suggestions for teaching method and modifications to meet
     various conditions, e.g. poorer ability pupils;
5   additional background material relevant to particular topics.

SYLLABUS

The course has been accepted by a number of Regional Examining
Boards as a CSE Mode 3 examination. It has also been accepted by
the Associated Examining Board as a Mode 3 GCE O-level examination.
During the period of school trials, and since, the course has been
successfully conducted on both a two-year and on a three-year basis.

The following syllabus indicates the areas which are likely to be
covered by the course, but should not be taken to indicate the
sequence in which the ground is covered in the programmed units.

Structures. Tension, compression, bending, torsion, rigidity in
two and three dimensions, moments, stability. Correct use of
members. Use of strain-gauging and photoelastic techniques.

Rotary motion. Spur, bevel, helical, and worm gears. Chains and
sprockets. Belts and pulleys. Gear trains (simple and compound).
Effect of gear ratio on torque produced. Velocity ratio. Mechanical advantage. Friction. Efficiency. Electric motor.
Characteristics of the permanent-magnet d.c. motor; speed/voltage,
load/current relationships. Work and energy as applied to the
electric motor and mechanical systems.

Linear motion. Mechanical - Crank and slider. Cams. Eccentrics.
                            Rack and pinion. Screw mechanisms.

                Electrical - Solenoids and electromagnets. Effect
                            of current and the number of turns.
                            Effect of varying the position of the
                            armature on the force produced by a
                            solenoid.

                Pneumatic - Single- and double-acting cylinders.
                            Effect of air pressure and piston
                            diameter on the force produced.

Basic electricity. Working knowledge of voltage, current, and
resistance. Ohm's law and simple calculations appropriate to
control devices.

Difference between a.c. and d.c.
The transformer. Half-wave and full-wave rectification. Simple
smoothing circuits.
Effect of current drain on the ripple of the rectified supply.
Protection devices - fuses, overload trips, earthing.

4

Use of electrical measuring instruments (voltmeter, ammeter, and ohmmeter).
Types, properties, and the use of capacitors - especially as applied to delay systems.
Series and parallel arrangements of cells, bulbs, resistors, and capacitors.
Introduction to electrical symbols and the diagrammatic representation of electrical circuits.
Resistance colour code, power rating, and tolerance.
Types of variable resistor - rheostat and potentiometer connections.
Effect of temperature on the resistance of metallic conductors with special reference to the filament lamp. Effect of temperature on carbon and semiconductor materials.
Checking of components for serviceability - resistors, capacitors, coils, diodes, and transistors.

<u>Switching - electrical</u>. Introduction to the common types of switch and their uses.

Toggle switches, push switches, microswitches, reed-switches, wafer switches.
The differing poles and 'ways' of the various types of switch.
The relay - methods of determining the energising and minimum hold-on currents.
Heavy-duty and multi-contact relays.
The uniselector.
The use of relays to produce oscillators, delays, and 'flip-flops'
The photocell as a switch.
Power dissipation in photocells.
Transistor circuits with special reference to the transistor as a switch.
The use of germanium and silicon diodes in switching circuits.

<u>Switching - pneumatic</u>. Manual, mechanical, electrical, low-pressure and high-pressure operated valves. The use of valves to produce delays and 'flip-flops'. The turbulence amplifier as a switch. Low-pressure sensing methods.

<u>Logic circuitry and applications</u>. AND, NAND, OR, and NOR arrangements. Truth tables, logic equations. Design of logical control systems, schematic diagrams of logic circuits. Safety circuitry for the protection of a machine and the operator. The use of manual switches, relays, pneumatic valves and electronic logic units in the logical control of apparatus and devices.

ESTIMATED COSTS

The equipment and quantities specified are those recommended for groups of 15 students. Schools have found, however, that when a second and a third group follow on in subsequent years, some duplication of particular items of equipment is desirable. This further expenditure will vary with timetabling arrangements and with the type of project work undertaken in the final year.

The total costs, ranging from £500 to £600, will depend upon whether or not additional items, such as power supply units and meters, are already available.

(Detailed information on the equipment requirements for this course can be obtained from The National Centre for School Technology, Trent Polytechnic, Burton Street, Nottingham NG1 4BU.)

CSE AND GCE O-LEVEL EXAMINATIONS

For a typical Mode 3, three-year examination course, the continuous assessment is provided by:

1 Set tests, under examination conditions:

  a) written - probably taken at the end of the second year and at the end of the first two terms in the final year.

  b) practical - at the end of the course;

2 Course work, with special reference to:

  a) notebooks recording the results of investigational assignment work and mini-projects,

  b) accounts of major projects.

(See Appendix 4 for specimen examination papers and further guidance.)

DISTINCTIVE FEATURES OF THE CONTROL TECHNOLOGY COURSE

The Control Technology course has been developed with the following considerations in mind.

a) <u>Many of the more important aspects of technology can be taught through an understanding of control principles</u>.

When a device is to be controlled, mechanised, or automated, a variety of restraints influence the final design. Typical constraints are the number of alternative solutions which can be considered in the light of previous experience, the ingenuity of the designer, the size of the installation, the cost, the speed of operation or repetition rate, environmental conditions such as excessive light or dust, types of sensor available, and so on.

The pupil working in the classroom or laboratory-workshop has

limited previous experience. Free of inhibitions, he has to rely
more on his ingenuity and inventiveness. There are potentially a
large number of alternative solutions to the control problems which
can arise in the school course; consequently the teacher should
encourage the pupils to accept the challenge of critically and
systematically examining each of their ideas. Because project work
is a regular feature of the course, groups of more than 15 pupils
will be difficult to handle by one teacher.

b) <u>Young people are naturally inventive.</u>

Many teachers feel that this inventiveness begins to decline
rapidly at about 13 years of age. The reasons for the decline are
probably complex, but for many pupils the decline may well be
linked with the tendency to 'spoon-feed' in some examination
subjects. This is brought about, some would say, by the syllabus
requirements.

The demands made upon the pupils in the Control Technology course,
together with the encouragement to experiment and devise solutions
to problems, help to maintain the flow of ideas. Not only is the
flow maintained, but the course encourages pupils to be practical
and realistic in putting forward solutions. Indeed, as the pupils
become familiar with the range of hardware available to them, and
acquire an understanding of the relevant principles, their solutions
more closely fit the specification.

c) <u>The course should be flexible</u>.

The structure and content of the course should reflect the fact
that technology is essentially a dynamic process. The latest
techniques and developments which are relevant to work at school
level can be incorporated by the enterprising teacher, especially
by way of minor and major projects.

The course has been written primarily for use by pupils of average
and above-average ability. An interesting and stimulating course
can also be provided for the less gifted by modifying some of the
assignments, leaving out others and using suitable replacements,
devising simple projects, and allowing more time throughout. It is
suggested, however, that the course be used at first in its original
form with able pupils, and subsequently modifications should be made.
Teachers may tend to underestimate, at first, the standard of work
attainable by their pupils: trials in various schools have shown
that, with sufficient motivation, high standards are possible with
pupils of lower ability.

The normal sequence of work for a three-year course* would be:

---

* Reference is made later in these notes to the possibility of a
  two-year course structure.

```
              ( Structures                    (including two mini-projects)
              ( Gears
1st year      ( Basic electricity
              ( Electrical switching
              ( A minor project - based on work to date

              ( Linear motion
              ( Pneumatic control
              ( Fluidic control (optional)
              ( Electronics
2nd year      (    - resistance
              (    - rectification
              (    - the transistor
              ( Logic circuits
              ( A project - of a half term or one term duration

3rd year      ( Any outstanding assignments
              ( A major project - one to two terms duration
```

Detailed guidance and suggestions are given in the Teachers' Notes for individual sections of the course. For example, it may be desirable for some pupils to omit certain assignments, or to post-pone them until others have been completed; alternatively, some teachers might wish to give greater emphasis to the work on Structures, for instance, by encouraging children to construct models from balsa wood and to test them to destruction.

Being sectionalised, parts of the course may be taken to enrich the work in other subjects. Teachers have already found that, in addition to teaching the Control Technology course proper, they can also use some of the methods and equipment to advantage in other areas, particularly on a modular-course basis.

d) <u>The Course must fit its objectives</u>.

Whether the course is used as it is presented or in some modified form, it is hoped that teachers will have certain objectives in mind. The course has stated objectives and many teachers will accept these, since they form a firm basis for the work in all its aspects.

Factors to be considered when teaching a modified version would include:

1 the relevance of the topics of the course to the stated objectives;

2 how well does the teaching method(s) used for a particular topic fulfil the objectives?

3 the relative importance of each objective as judged by the teacher;

4 is an objective determined by consideration of general education or vocationally-directed education?

5 How much emphasis is given to each objective
   i) by virtue of the course content?
   ii) by virtue of the relative frequency of the methods used to teach the various topics?

e) The equipment should be reliable, easy and rapid to assemble, attractive, and compatible.

The electrical equipment is housed in attractive units; electrical connections being made through 4mm sockets and stackable plugs. The soldering of wires, except in major project work, has been avoided in order that circuitry can be made up quickly. By using the units, with connecting leads, quite complex circuit arrangements can be set up in minutes. Should a design fault or limitation become evident, the arrangement can be dismantled and an alternative method tried again in a very short time.

All the electrical equipment has been selected in order to be operated from 12 volt d.c. supplies. When alternative equipment to that recommended is being considered, teachers should ensure that the units will operate under all the required conditions, as indicated in the assignment sheets. For instance, a different photocell may not operate the relay unit or, alternatively, a different type of relay may not operate from the photocell satisfactorily under the conditions assumed in the assignment. Any new units introduced should also operate satisfactorily on 12 volts d.c. supplies.

Surplus equipment - industrial and military - is a useful source of 'hardware' and components for projects in the Course. There may be a temptation to use complete units but, whilst occasionally this may be desirable, in general such equipment is more valuable as a source of 'bits and pieces'. Assuming that a suitable store is available, this equipment is probably best left intact until specific components are required by pupils for a major project.

TEACHING METHODS

The subject matter of the course is generally taught by a combination of four different methods:

1 programmed or sequential assignments and follow-up sheets,

2 teacher demonstrations,

3 homework questions and assignments,

4 project work.

Programmed assignments

The assignment method of teaching is used for the following reasons:

1 It ensures that all children cover the same basic material.

2 It enables pupils to work at their own pace. Some pupils obviously work faster than others and, since most of the principles are learned through experiment and investigation, adequate time must be available to allow for different rates of working.

3 The follow-up sheets contain additional information, some of which is 'for information only' and would not warrant discussion time. In effect, some of the information in the follow-up sheets is used as one uses a textbook. The majority of teachers involved in school trials, however, felt strongly that the follow-up sheets should not be made available to pupils until they had spent sufficient time working unaided on the assignments.

The teacher should visit each group of pupils as they work, to discuss and to check progress. He should ensure that full answers are written, as indicated by the questions and statements printed in bold italic type in the assignments, and also that suitable notes are made from the follow-up sheets. These notes should include points which have not been understood as pupils have worked through the assignments and also the important additional information not referred to in the assignment.

Should pupils make errors as a result of misunderstanding of basic principles met previously, they should be encouraged to refer back to their notes or to the appropriate assignment. All pupils will meet difficulties from time to time, and the advantage of making suitable notes will quickly become apparent to most. The teacher should avoid providing complete answers, but should direct pupils to the source of the answer.

Teacher demonstrations

A number of these are covered in the teachers' notes, but as the teacher becomes familiar with the course he will no doubt devise others. Although buffer experiments are suggested from time to time, in order to extend the faster and brighter pupils, it is possible that timing difficulties will still be experienced with mixed-ability groups. Should too wide a gap arise between groups or individuals, the teacher should use his discretion and demonstrate certain assignments to help bring the group level. Such demonstrations may also be necessary because of a shortage of apparatus on occasions.

Homework assignments and questions

Many schools will allocate some homework time to pupils who are
taking the Control Technology course. Such time is valuable, for
it allows pupils to work through assignments in class and, for
homework, write up the notes and/or answer homework questions.

Project Work

In the early stages of the course, pupils require considerable
guidance in project work. The initial projects, therefore, occur
as part of the assignments, and pupils tackle the problems in a
planned sequence. In later project work it is recommended that
pupils are reminded, from time to time, of the notes 'Guide to
Project Work' at the end of the assignments book. Four different
types of projects are suggested for inclusion in the assignments,

1 Mini-projects. These are the projects specified in the assignments, e.g. the design and construction of a bridge, or the
   design and construction of a lifting device. In this kind of
   project, a suitable specification is given and the solution is
   closely related to recently completed assignments. Materials -
   mainly Meccano and the basic electrical units. Time required -
   two or three double periods. (Two or three pupils per group.)

2 Minor projects. These projects are usually attempted after the
   Electrical-switching Assignments. Pupils are given a list of
   possible project titles (not a strict specification) from which
   they choose one. Alternatively, if they wish, pupils can suggest
   their own subject. Ideally, the problem and the solution should
   be related to all the assignments completed up to that time.
   When all the projects are completed, it is helpful if a member
   of each group describes and explains their project solution to
   the others. Materials - primarily the quick-assembly units.
   Time required - four to six double periods. (Two or three pupils
   per group.)

3 Major projects. These are usually attempted after the Linear-
   motion and the Pneumatic-control Assignments. Here the same
   specification might well be given to all the groups. Each pupil
   is asked to consider several solutions and to select the most
   satisfactory; it is then possible to group together those pupils
   who are hoping to make use of similar principles or methods. The
   pupils in the group then select the best solution or combination
   of solutions. Materials - a wider range of materials, including
   Perspex, wood, Meccano, and any control devices. Pupils should
   be discouraged, perhaps, from using only the quick-assembly
   units. Time - between half a term and a full term. (Two or
   three pupils per group.)

4 Major group project. It is suggested that, in the final year,
groups should design and manufacture a device to meet their own
agreed specification. At this stage it is sometimes an advantage
to elect a 'foreman' who will allocate responsibilities to the
various members of the group. The role of 'foreman' can be shared
to allow others to gain experience, but several periods must be
devoted to discussion and initial design planning. Materials -
practically all materials; construction should not be limited to
quick-assembly units and methods.

The Teacher's Role in Project Work

It cannot be emphasised too strongly that in this course all
projects should be primarily the work of the pupils and not that
of the teacher. When organising the project work, the teacher has,
perhaps, three main functions:

1 to act as a supplier of material, equipment, and components
   appropriate to the project;
2 to provide a stabilising influence throughout, and to ensure
   that a project is feasible, technically and financially;
3 to provide advice and guidance on which pupils can rely,
   particularly when they are unsure of basic principles.

The teacher's main function, then, during the design and construction of a project, is to check that principles are being applied
correctly. If he is doing much more than this, then the pupils
could become, at worst, mere labourers for the realisation of his
ideas. As the project is completed, it should have developed from
the pupil's ideas. This must not be confused, however, with the
fact that sometimes a teacher may have made part of a device. If
he has done so, it should have been at the request of the pupil and
to meet a specific need.

WHERE DOES CONTROL TECHNOLOGY FIT INTO THE CURRICULUM?

The course is designed primarily for boys and girls of average and
above-average ability. It will normally be of three-years
duration, with pupils taking the course from 13 to 16 years of age.
Based on a timetable of 40 minute periods, a typical time allocation would be:

Year 1   one double period

Year 2   two double periods and one single period
            (or one triple)

Year 3   two double periods and one single period
            (or one triple)

Some schools have found that a two-year course is possible, since
most of the third year is devoted to a major project. In this case,

12

more emphasis should be given to projects in the second year, possibly at the expense of some of the assignments.

The Control Technology course was not intended to be an alternative to either science or craft work, but has been developed as a course which is complementary to both. Although it is not essential, it is desirable that pupils have some basic knowledge of physics and of craftwork before starting the course.

For convenience in some schools, Control Technology has been fitted into craft or technical-studies option schemes, or even into craft-plus-science option schemes, causing little disturbance to the rest of the curriculum.

Teachers with an interest in technology are usually to be found in physics or technical departments, and it is, therefore, mainly from these disciplines that the teachers of Control Technology emerge. Experience has shown that ideally there should be at least one member from each department willing to contribute, since both will have specialised knowledge and experience of value.

CLASSROOM, WORKSHOP, OR LABORATORY?

A room with the following facilities is required:

1 an adequate number of mains electrical power sockets,
2 a bench or pillar drilling machine,
3 a portable electric drill,
4 two sets of twist drills (limited range),
5 at least five 12 volt d.c., 5A power-supply units.

The following are also recommended:

6 storage space for 'ex-equipment' items and components etc.,
7 storage space for unfinished projects,
8 storage space for quick-assembly units, Meccano, pneumatic equipment, etc.,
9 an air compressor,
10 storage space for paper, books, and miscellaneous items.

PROJECT SUGGESTIONS

(Minor projects undertaken after Electrical-switching assignments)

1 Various burglar alarms
2 Bridge which automatically lifts as a vehicle approaches
3 Warning device for an over-weight load approaching a bridge
4 Device for removing articles of above standard height from a conveyor
5 Automatic flashing light for given variable lengths of time
6 Device for counting the number of vehicles crossing a bridge
7 An automatic 'scarecrow'

8   An electrical lock for a safe or cupboard
9   Safety devices to be fitted to a fairground roundabout
10 Rain detector
11 Sorting machine for coloured balls
12 Traffic-light control system
13 Automatic turntable for model locomotive
14 Automatic level-crossing gates
15 Liquid-level indicator
16 Device for counting the number of people entering a room, but
    not those leaving
17 Circuit for a quiz game, to indicate which team first pressed
    the button
18 Automatic garage door

Some Suggestions for Major Projects

Warning devices: 'Low bridge' warning system
                           Motorway speed indicator

Dispensing devices: Delivery of correct quantities –
                           e.g. marbles, nuts and bolts, liquids

Sorting devices: Selecting objects of different width,
                           length, or colour
                           Selecting components according to their
                           properties, e.g. selecting good or
                           rejecting faulty diodes

Repetition Devices: Drilling holes in blocks of wood
(sequence switching)   Drilling equally spaced holes in
                           metal strip

Repetition devices: Drink dispenser
(programmed)   Automatic gantry crane
                           Automatic metal-plating equipment

Display devices: Lighting of bulbs to indicate a sequence
                           Lights indicating information
                           Electrical indicator board for school
                             timetable display
                           'Random' light display
                           Digital display for scoreboard

'Reaction' devices: Automatic control of a swing bridge
                           White-line follower
                           Quiz-game reaction indicator
                           Constant-level reservoir

Selection devices: School 'pupil-finder' punched-card-
                           operated display
                           Telephone exchange for school
                           Equipment for the disabled

14

★ All of these projects have been undertaken by pupils involved in Control Technology examination courses.

THE CONTROL TECHNOLOGY APPROACH TO PROJECT WORK

1 All pupils work through a programmed basic course which develops the ability to solve problems with little help from the teacher.

2 Progressive training is given in the approach to project work (see note on the types of project).

3 Quick, easy to use, and reliable equipment allows pupils to test their ideas before time-consuming practical work is undertaken.

Using this equipment, pupils gain confidence and achieve regular success.

4 Quick-construction methods are used whenever possible, e.g. basic electrical units, Meccano, etc. This allows a number of modifications to be made, if necessary, in the minimum of time.

5 The content of the basic course permits many stimulating projects to be set - projects naturally grow out of the course.

6 The solution to the project is initially unknown, with the pupils having to start from first principles. Solutions are rarely to be found in textbooks.

SOME PROBLEMS ENCOUNTERED IN PROJECT WORK

1 The difficulty of choosing a suitable topic.

2 The pupil's limited knowledge. Difficulty may be encountered in locating sources of information, resulting in unfortunate delay. The information may be too advanced for the pupil to understand or apply.

3 Availability of specialist techniques, equipment, and materials.

4 Pupils' lack of experience in the whole approach to project work.

5 Some project work involves little problem-solving - the pupil may begin with a pre-conceived solution.

6 The initial stages of some projects are the most difficult, because decisions taken in the first few weeks often determine later work.

7   A team-teaching approach is often desirable when knowledge and
    guidance in various fields are necessary.

8   Repeated failure or frustration can affect morale. A measure
    of success is normally required.

THE TEACHER'S ROLE IN PROJECT WORK

1   The project must be primarily the pupil's work and not the
    teacher's. Too much intervention by the teacher can seriously
    reduce the educational value of this portion of the course.

2   When pupils need correction, the teacher should correct, if
    possible with regard to principles only, by referring pupils
    to their previous assignment notes.

3   The teacher should ensure, as far as possible, that:
    a)   the project is a suitable one,
    b)   the proposed solutions are feasible, in order that pupils
         avoid having to make too many unsuccessful attempts.

4   The teacher should provide advice and guidance, together with
    appropriate resources - components, materials, equipment, etc.-
    when asked.

THE RECORDING OF PROJECT WORK

The thorough recording of project work is important:

a)   because pupils will need to refer back to their previous work,
     particularly when problems are encountered;

b)   for examination assessment purposes. The written account is
     often all that exists of the project, which may have been
     dismantled after completion and testing.

The following guidance may help in the recording of project work:

1   It is essential that a record is made as the work progresses.

2   A range of alternative solutions should be considered. This
    advice must be stressed, otherwise pupils will be content to
    develop their initial, often mediocre, ideas.

3   The reasons for adopting a particular solution should be noted.

4   When modifications are needed later, the reasons for these
    should be given. This is often the only way of knowing that
    other work was carried out, once the project is completed.

5   A concluding section should indicate how well the project fulfils the specification. When a project is only partly successful, an investigation into the causes of failure should be carried out and briefly recorded.

6   Precise recording is essential. The use of appropriate line-diagrams, freehand sketching, and photographs should be encouraged. Descriptions can be in concise note form.

The adequate recording of project work is largely a question of habit; therefore guidance should be given by the teacher to ensure that suitable recording is carried out as the work progresses. A little time at the end of most lessons can be used to record the progress made.

PROJECT ROUTE

THE APPROACH TO A PROJECT

In the early stages of many projects, the pupils may start with
rather vague general ideas and suggestions - for example, special
equipment for use by the disabled - then, after a period of
research, they should formulate their own appropriate project
specification.

The following example, however, has been chosen to illustrate the
manner in which a wide range of solutions should be considered in
many Control Technology projects. The specification might be
worded in this case, as, 'To design and construct a dispensing
machine to place, repeatedly, ten marbles into suitable containers.

The device would appear to require four distinct parts or units:

1   a marble-feed mechanism,
2   a method by which the correct number of marbles is selected,
3   a system to deliver the marbles to the container,
4   the provision of containers in the right place at the correct
    time.

If each problem is broken down into its essential parts, a number
of different ideas can be developed for each part. (Ideally each
solution should make use of a different principle, rather than
involve the minor modification of a previous idea.)

Some possible solutions

1   MARBLE FEED MECHANISM

marble carried
in the hole

stationary disc
with one hole
through which
marbles full one
at a time

(a)
angled, rotating tray
with hole(s) near periphery

rotating cone inside the
drum to 'agitate' the marbles
(probably erratic in operation)

(b)

hole for the
delivery of marbles

a rocking mechanism
releases one marble
at a time

(c)

the spring-loaded stop is moved
clear of the column to allow
another marble to drop as the
feed mechanism returns

(d)

2   QUANTITY-SELECTING DEVICE

(a) By weight

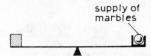

supply of
marbles

with the correct quantity of
marbles the balance will tip

(only reliable if the marbles
have very similar masses)

(b) By measurement of a column

stop A moves down
stop B lifts to release the correct quantity
stop B returns
stop A lifts to allow more marbles to pass

(only reliable if the marbles
have very similar diameters)

(c) By counting

each marble is counted individually;
when the correct quantity has
passed, the feed is cut off while
the container is replaced

3   DELIVERY SYSTEM

the stop lifts to allow
the marbles into the box

the angle tilts to discharge
the marbles which are
guided into the box

(a)

(b)

hinged side of box allows
marbles to be discharged

(c)

4   PROVISION OF CONTAINERS

roller
feed

when the box is filled
it is pushed away at
right angles to allow
another to take its place

19

the conveyor belt stops when the box is opposite the delivery system and is restarted when the box has received the desired quantity

Each proposal should be analysed and evaluated (this often requires the building of models or 'rigs' to test ideas) and the most suitable solution to each part is selected and the reason is given.

The choice may be modified when the system is examined as a whole. One selected method may be best operated electrically, and another pneumatically; generally it is advisable to limit the power sources to be used on grounds of cost and convenience. Obviously it is essential that all the parts in the final design are compatible.

Each idea must now be developed. Ideally, detailed drawings should be made before construction work is commenced; however, some pupils have difficulty in expressing three-dimensional forms on paper, and interest may decline if the teacher always insists on suitable drawings. Indeed, in some circumstances it may be better to let pupils start constructional work without detailed drawings, when working with materials and equipment which allow modifications to be made as the work progresses. It is likely that modifications will have to be made during the construction and testing stages. These changes should be recorded and explained.

The pupil's evaluation of his project is most important; a critical appraisal should be attempted whenever possible. Avoid undue discouragement from the project which has failed: an analysis of the reasons for failure, and perhaps an attempt to correct the faults, can be of more value than the project which is only marginally better but, since it performs satisfactorily, is not viewed as critically.

In a group project it is important that all pupils are involved in major decisions and have an overall understanding of the project. To disseminate information on the details of a project, the use of an overhead projector has been found helpful. Each pupil is able to outline his individual contribution, and others in the group can then extract the information they consider necessary to produce an adequate project write-up.

Guidance notes

INTRODUCTION

The following notes are intended to be used in conjunction with the pupils' materials for the Control Technology course. An effort has been made to lighten the teacher's burden, with regard to preparation for the teaching of each programme, by dividing the notes into clearly defined sections. It is hoped that, before introducing a particular programme to his pupils for the first time, the teacher will carefully read through each section of the notes. These notes will give an overall picture of what is involved in the relevant programme and how the programme relates to those which follow. Instructions on the construction and use of demonstration apparatus are included.

The following five aspects are usually covered.

a) Guidance notes. These include the aims to be considered for a particular programme. Some of the material and a number of the explanations given in the Teachers' Notes are intended primarily to be of benefit to the teacher; however, a capable group of pupils might be able to cover some of the extra work, in which case periodic class discussions could be fruitful.

b) A list of apparatus required for fifteen pupils, giving five groups of three.

c) Demonstrations which might be used preceding or following the actual programme. The equipment and its use is described, but constructional details are given separately, where appropriate.

It is not anticipated that all demonstrations will be given quite as suggested. The teacher is expected to select and to use only those demonstrations which he feels will be effective. In some circumstances the teacher may decide to present the problem to the whole group, or alternatively he may set the challenge to a competent group who will later demonstrate their findings.

d) Buffer experiments. The use of programmed notes reveals the need for buffer experiments, since bright pupils will obviously work faster than others. In most cases, these experiments will be extensions of those suggested in the programme.

e) Homework questions. A period of homework is often desirable, even if this consists of recording the work done in class. Some teachers may welcome typical questions appropriate to the programme.

21

Note: In order to assist pupils (and teachers) in determining when work should be recorded in notebooks, certain sentences in the assignments are printed in bold italic type. This is intended to indicate that a permanent record should be kept. This method is not used in follow-ups, since it is anticipated that pupils will record anything mentioned in them which they have not already fully noted or understood.

Structures

The main purpose of this section of the course is to enable the
pupils to use materials intelligently and efficiently. We cannot
assume that pupils will initially be able to use Meccano to produce
rigid structures. Briefly, the programme is arranged to introduce
to the children some ideas about triangular formation of members,
tension forces, compression forces, the forces involved in a member
which is under bending, and the stability of structures. Such
information is needed, since, although we need not place undue
emphasis upon craftsmanship, the rigidity of a structure is vital,
particularly when a device containing moving parts is to function
satisfactorily.

STRUCTURES ASSIGNMENT 1

Here we are asking the children to fasten together four pieces of
Meccano strip and to test the arrangement for rigidity in one plane.
(It should be remembered that when we ask, 'Is the structure
rigid?', we are concerned with only two dimensions. Obviously we
should not discourage anyone who wishes to extend this to three
dimensions.)

Several solutions apart from fastening the strip across opposite
corners will be suggested, but we should emphasise that triangulation provides the best solution.

At the end of <u>Structures Follow-up 1</u>, the pupils are asked to
consider which kind of brace is the most suitable for producing a
rigid structure. After allowing sufficient time for thought,
possibly by waiting until the next lesson, the teacher could:

a) demonstrate the best solution (see section on demonstrations);
b) explain why one solution is preferable to the others.
Suggestions for further demonstrations are also mentioned.

<u>Follow-up 1</u> shows the Warren girder, and teachers should at this
stage have available clear photographs or drawings to illustrate
that the arrangement is indeed used extensively for bridges, cranes,
and other structures.

A period of discussion should follow, in which questions of
stability and moments may well be put forward by pupils as an
introduction to work which follows later. In any discussion
arising out of the programme, we should avoid giving too many
answers but should leave some matters for further consideration.

Apparatus required (15 pupils, 5 groups of 3)

The quadrilaterals can be made from any lengths of Meccano <u>flat</u>
strips. At least 20 pieces are therefore required initially.
Additional lengths of flat strip, corner brackets, and gussets will
also be needed for making the structures rigid.

Hence the apparatus required is:

    assorted Meccano flat strip,
    some corner brackets (part no.133),
    Meccano nuts and bolts,
    means of applying forces (other than by hand), e.g. string,
       spring-balances, and weights.

One of our aims in this course should be to make pupils think and
formulate their own solutions to problems. It is easy to present
the solution by making a statement or suggestion at an early stage,
or by providing a set of components carefully selected to solve the
problem.

To avoid the latter, the following alternative suggestions may be
useful regarding the supply of components during a lesson.

1 Give pupils free access to a range of Meccano parts. Let them
   select any component which they wish to use to solve their
   problems.

2 Even if it is necessary to limit the amount of Meccano for the
   lesson, ensure that, in addition to those parts required to
   solve the problem, other Meccano parts are included so that a
   certain amount of selection and rejection is required. Flat
   strips and nuts and bolts to make the quadrilaterals could be
   made available at the beginning of the lesson, whilst other
   parts - such as more flat strips, corner brackets, and gussets -
   could be withheld until the design work has been completed on
   paper.

Demonstrations

Photographs of bridges, cranes, etc., showing the use of triangulation can be introduced at this stage. These might be followed by
the four demonstrations to show the best bracing method.

DEMONSTRATION A

Construct a framework as shown below:

no. 1a (19-hole flat strip)

nut and bolt

no.5 (5-hole flat strip)

no.12c
(2-hole obtuse
angle bracket)

no. 12 (2-hole angle bracket)

Apply forces, by hand, at the opposite corners (i.e. push or pull). The corners will retain their original shape, but the long side members will bend easily.

The amount of bending will depend upon a number of factors, some of which can be difficult to explain, and teachers may wish to study texts on Structures to learn more about the subject.

The following diagram shows the distorted structure and the forces in the individual members.

T = tension
C = compression
B = bending

It is not suggested that the kinds of forces existing in the various members should be discussed fully with pupils, since this is covered later.

DEMONSTRATION B

Construct a framework as shown below:

no. 8a

nut and bolt

no. 1 (25-hole flat strip)

no. 8b

no. 12

2 of no. 12

Apply forces to W and Y as shown.

Very much larger forces are now required to produce any
appreciable distortion of the side members, showing this to be a
much better solution. The explanation for this is that all the
members in the framework are either in tension or compression only.
Bending of side members occurs as a result of excessive compressive forces. The forces in this structure are along the length
of a member, and only when the compressive forces, in a 'perfectly'
straight member, cause dislocation in the structure of the material
will bending occur. (In practice a member is never quite 'straight'
and bending occurs with modest forces.)

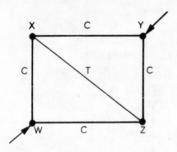

DEMONSTRATION C

The following demonstration will emphasise the difference between bending in pin-jointed structures and bending caused by forces other than those applied along the length of a member.

Hold a length of flat strip at one end by clamping to a bench, allowing most of the length to overhang. Show that (a) no amount of 'pulling' (tension forces) will cause bending, (b) very large 'push' forces (compression) are needed to cause bending, and (c) a finger pushing at right angles to the strip easily causes bending.

Here we are simulating what happens in the following:

DEMONSTRATION D

From photoelastic material, cut strips 12mm wide (take care not to stress it by clamping etc. - see appendix 1) and construct two right angle supports as shown.

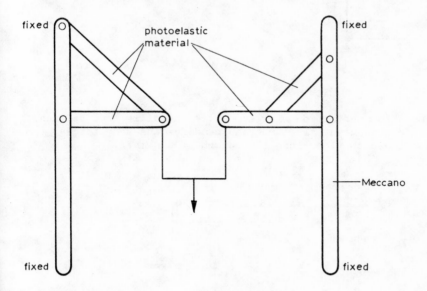

This demonstration is most effective if both arrangements, when similarly loaded, can be viewed simultaneously. This is possible with the apparatus described in appendix 1.

Special equipment - photoelastic stress analysis apparatus (for construction details and brief notes see appendix 1).

It may be helpful to use this apparatus to provide further evidence that the solution shown in Demonstration B is better than that shown in A. As the apparatus will be used again in Structures 3 to demonstrate the forces acting in a loaded beam, Demonstration D could be delayed until then and used to recall and reinforce the work of the first section.

Possibly the easiest way to explain the pattern formed in photo-elastic material when stressed is to compare the lines (fringes) with the contour lines on a map. Where there are many lines close together (mountains), the structure is highly stressed; if there are few lines, the stress is low; if the colour is the same throughout, the stress is evenly distributed.

On loading the two structures, more fringes will appear in the structure on the right - particularly in the horizontal member, as

this is in bending. The short supporting member is also highly
stressed in tension.

In the pin-jointed structure on the left, the members are less
highly stressed and are in either compression or tension.

Buffer Experiments

1 Repeat the programme using an entirely different shape of
   structure, and compare the results with the first shape.
2 Take measurements of the forces needed to distort the structure,
   with and without reinforcement, using spring-balances.

Homework Question

1 Examine the construction of electricity pylons, cranes, and
   bridges to see how the principle of triangulation is applied.
   Make sketches in your notebook.

STRUCTURES ASSIGNMENT 2

We now approach the problem of three-dimensional structures. The
pupils are asked to construct a box-like structure entirely from
flat strip. They are asked to check the rigidity of the structure.
They will notice that the vertical sides will bend either inwards
or outwards under a vertical load, and that any force sideways will
cause distortion of the shape as the members pivot about the
securing bolts. With their knowledge of triangulation, pupils
should then attempt to achieve some rigidity. At this stage they
must be aware of the various Meccano parts available. Angle
girders could be used for the vertical members, to give greater
rigidity.

We should emphasise here, and elsewhere in the course, that when
designing full-size structures other factors besides strength have
to be considered. These include the weight, transport and assembly
problems, and the cost of the final product.

The programme does not suggest methods of loading the structure
when it is being tested, so we might encourage them to use their
ingenuity. Whilst no given load is specified, when completed, the
improved structure should at least be capable of taking the full
weight of a standing pupil. The 'balancing act' will inevitably
produce sideways forces as well as vertical; obviously the teacher
must keep a careful watch to prevent serious damage to parts.

Apparatus Required (five groups)

For the construction of the tower illustrated in Structures 2, the following Meccano parts are required:

An assortment of flat strip (at least 20 long strips and 20 short ones),
Double angle strips,
Meccano nuts and bolts.

The use of long supporting strips (part no.1 - 320mm) indicates bending most effectively.

As suggested in the notes, these vertical strips should be replaced with angle girders if a really satisfactory solution is to be obtained.

Other parts required to carry out modifications:

long angle girders
assorted flat strip or angle girders for cross-bracing

Demonstrations

1 Photographs of tower cranes etc showing their construction.
2 The teacher should construct a tower showing an acceptable solution. He should demonstrate that it will withstand a pupil's weight and perhaps his own.

Possible solution:

Buffer Experiments

Devise other methods of applying and measuring forces. Some pupils could undertake a quantitative analysis.

Homework Questions

1 The diagram shows a tower (not very rigid) made from strips of steel bolted at the corners. A platform is placed on the top of the tower and a 100kg load is applied centrally as shown.

   a) Are the vertical members in tension, compression, or bending? Explain your answer.

   b) If the force was increased gradually, what do you expect would happen to the vertical members?

   c) Are there any forces in the eight horizontal members and, if so, are they forces of tension or compression?

   d) If you had a means of measuring the forces in each of the vertical members, what force would you expect to find in each?

2 The diagrams (a),(b),(c),and (d) show a simple tower with the vertical members made from flat strip. A platform is placed on top of the tower, and forces are applied in the directions shown by the arrows.

   a) Assuming that the two forces are equal, say what you would expect to happen to the two vertical members X and Y in each of the diagrams.

   b) In diagram b, the two forces shown could be replaced by two forces at right angles to one another (not parallel to one another as shown) and still have a similar effect. Draw a diagram showing these two new forces.

STRUCTURES ASSIGNMENT 3

This mini-project, which may take two to three lessons to complete, enables pupils to put into practice what they have discovered in Structures 1 and 2. The specification given may be changed to suit the available materials. The important part of the project, however, is to restrict construction to the use of lengths of Meccano which are short compared with the bridge span itself, thus ensuring that triangulation and the correct kind of section is used.

A fast-working group could investigate the forces acting on the ends of the bridge (reactions). This should be followed by a demonstration to show the principle of moments.

Before embarking on the project, it is helpful to suggest to pupils an approach to project work to ensure logical procedure. The following is offered as a guide and appears in the Pupils' Assignment book.

THE APPROACH TO PROJECT WORK

The words here underlined indicate the need for a written record of the work.

1 State the problem precisely.

2 Outline several possible solutions.

3 Choose one solution and say why you chose it in preference to any other.

4 Divide the problem into several separate sections. Work on each independently, keeping in mind that all sections must fit together.

5 With the aid of sketches make a plan of how you intend solving each section of the project.

6 Suggest any modifications during or after construction.

7 Test the items which have been constructed. Say where your design has succeeded - and how well - and where it has failed.

8 Suggest further modifications for improvement. These may or may not be carried out.

The above procedure helps to illustrate that success can follow initial failure. We encourage pupils to have a positive attitude by analysing the situation to discover the reasons for failure.

It is recommended that the pupils should keep fairly rigidly to a pattern of this sort, otherwise poor quality reports will result. As the course progresses, it is hoped that pupils will also realise the importance of a written record. Later work will emphasise this

point, since they will find that they cannot progress rapidly
unless they can refer back to previous work, particularly circuit
diagrams. The procedure will also encourage them to approach a
problem logically, thus eliminating guesswork.

Pupils will need considerable guidance to enable them to express
their thoughts visually. Sketches should be of a simple nature,
so that ideas can be shown quickly and clearly. It is felt that
engineering-drawing techniques are inappropriate because:

a) additional special equipment (and space) would be required;
b) progress would be slow because advanced techniques would have
   to be taught, and much time would be spent in making accurate
   drawings of ideas, many of which would be rejected before the
   drawings were completed;
c) very sophisticated techniques are needed to represent satisfactorily the complex arrangements developed in later work.

However, simple line diagrams are not always satisfactory, as they
become very confusing when showing complex three-dimensional
shapes.

Apparatus Required

In addition to a variety of Meccano strip, angle girder, and nuts
and bolts, some strip material would help to make the bridge deck
more realistic.

A simple design will need approximately twenty to thirty pieces of
Meccano. It might be advisable to check the number of parts
available before starting this programme, and if necessary reduce
the number of groups.

Special Demonstrations

1 DEMONSTRATIONS TO SHOW THE FORCES ACTING IN A LOADED, END-
   SUPPORTED BEAM.

a) <u>Rubber-model demonstration</u>
   A block of rubber approximately 225mm long, 50mm wide and 25mm
   thick is used.

saw cuts 5mm spacing,
approx. 3mm deep

When loaded, the rubber bends as shown. The distortion of the saw cuts clearly demonstrates the tensile and compressive forces present. The cuts in the lower half open up considerably, indicating tension; and in the upper half the saw cuts close up, showing compression.

b) <u>Photoelastic stress analysis demonstration</u>
   Equipment required: photoelastic analysis apparatus (appendix 1);
   strip of photoelastic material approx 225 x 12 x 3mm;
   four 4mm diameter holes drilled as shown.

By applying the load from the two points A and B, circular bending is obtained.

When the strip is loaded, a dark line appears approximately along the centre line of the strip (this indicates the neutral axis), and fringes appear above and below the line; the greater the load, the greater the number of fringes.

34

From the patterns produced, it is difficult to determine which fringes indicate tensile forces and which indicate compressive forces, so it is suggested that reference is made to the previous rubber-model demonstration.

c) Strain-gauge techniques
   Equipment required (see appendix 2): Perspex angle 12 x 12 x 3mm with strain-gauge attached.

4 mm plugs

strain-gauge cemented in position

Sellotape for protection

two strips of Perspex cemented together to produce angle

Using the Perspex angle with the strain-gauge attached, insert the 4mm plugs and zero the instrument as described in appendix 2.

Tension the angle by pulling on each end. Notice in which direction the pointer moves.

Next place the angle vertically, and press on the end to produce compression. The pointer now moves in the opposite direction.

Further demonstrations could show that the internal forces in the member might change if the external forces were applied in different positions, e.g., a cantilever.

tension

compression

2 DEMONSTRATION TO INDICATE TENSION OR COMPRESSION IN INDIVIDUAL
   MEMBERS OF A STRUCTURE

Pupils were asked to indicate, on the sketches of their final
design, the forces acting in individual members of the structure.

It is fairly easy to do this for certain members, but more
difficult for others. If the load is moved, the forces acting
in particular members may change from tensile to compressive and
vice versa.

To indicate clearly whether a member is in tension or compression, strain-gauging techniques can be used. The Meccano
member under investigation would be removed and replaced with
the Perspex angle girder to which is attached a strain-gauge.

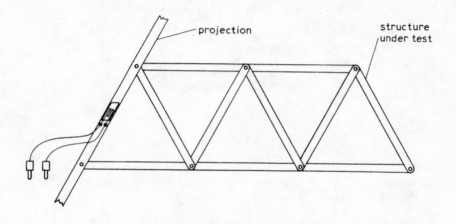

The strain-gauge is connected to the instrument, the meter is
adjusted to zero, and the load is then applied. The direction
of movement of the pointer indicates whether the member is in
tension or compression.

The meter indicates not only the type of force, but also the
magnitude of the force.

Buffer Experiments

Use two spring-balances to support the bridge. From this the
pupils should discover that:

    the total upward force = the total downward force

spring-
balance

spring-
balance

(reaction)

A teacher demonstration could then be given to illustrate the principle of moments by moving the load along the bridge.

Homework Questions

1 If the child has a mass of 30kg what is the tension in each rope? (Neglect the mass of the seat and ropes.)

2 If two boys, A and B, carry a mass of 100kg placed upon a pole, as shown, find the proportion of the mass carried by each boy. (Neglect the mass of the pole.)

2m   3m

A

100 kg

B

3   Indicate with a 'C' those members in compression and with a 'T'
    those members in tension in figs (a) to (e) below. If a member
    is in bending, indicate this also, showing which side is in
    compression and which in tension.

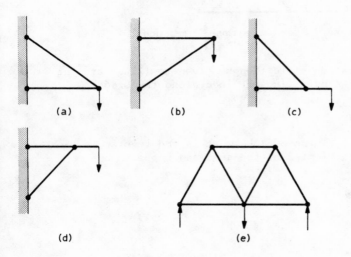

(a)   (b)   (c)

(d)   (e)

STRUCTURES ASSIGNMENT 4

A further mini-project is now suggested in which pupils are
expected to apply principles which they have already learned and to
consider the problem of stability of free-standing devices. A
specification is given for a lifting device for loading vehicles.
Again we emphasise the importance of design on paper before construction takes place. We now bring in consideration of the cost
and weight of such a structure by asking that the final design
shall be as stable and as rigid as possible without incorporating
unnecessary members.

Most pupils realise that a member under tension can be replaced by
wire supports, and some interesting devices can be produced using
a number of wire supports in place of flat strip. Interesting
discussion points also arise as to the possibility of constructing
a crane completely from wire (i.e. all members under tension). As
the teacher goes round the various groups, he should ask questions
such as, 'Is that member under tension or compression?', or, 'Have
you included any members which are unnecessary?'

An assortment of lengths of wire with bolts at each end for
securing them rigidly to the structure could be made available.
Cut a number of different lengths of wire of about 26s.w.g. Drill

38

a hole in the head of a Meccano bolt, as shown, thread the wire
through the hole, and twist.

The teacher may feel it wise to wait until definite lengths are
requested, and to have long lengths of wire and a supply of ready-
drilled bolts available. The ends should be well twisted to
prevent slipping.

As each model is completed, the teacher should comment on the
result, perhaps offering further suggestions. These suggestions,
however, should be carefully worded. For instance we might say,
'Are you sure that this member should be made from flat strip?',
but never, 'This member is under tension so it must be made from
flat strip rather than angle, to reduce the weight of the crane.'
In short, questions should be phrased in such a way that the
answers come from the pupils. Pupils must be confident that they
know why their device is made the way it is. Later, when the
pupils start major projects, it is all too easy for the teacher to
provide solutions to the problems which arise.

Only when the model has been satisfactorily completed should
reference be made to the follow-up sheet.

Apparatus Required   (15 pupils, 5 groups of 3)

    Assorted Meccano angle girder and strip, flanged plates, etc
    five lengths of cord and hooks
    five Meccano motors
    assorted gears
    five 1kg weights
    assorted pulleys for cord
    short axles

Some teachers may wish to have a model vehicle available.

Demonstrations

The work should be followed by demonstrations to consolidate the
understanding of tension, compression, bending, and torsion.
Demonstrations including photoelastic stress analysis and strain-
gauge techniques, if not already covered, could now be given.

If necessary, demonstrate the effect of moments by placing weights
at various distances from the pivot of a see-saw arrangement.

Buffer Experiments

Whenever pupils are attempting assignments involving the design and construction of a device, the faster groups can be extended by encouraging them to make their device more reliable or sophisticated.

Homework Questions

1 What vertical force will be required at X to prevent the crane from overturning?

2m   8m

2 At what distance from the axis of rotation should the centre of the balancing mass be placed? (Neglect the mass of the structure.)

25 m

10000 kg

3 Analyse the forces acting in the members of this structure and indicate with 'C' and 'T' whether they are in compression or tension.

Gears

The work already covered in the Structures section results in the
production of more or less static mini-projects. The Gears
assignments are concerned with motion and the transmission of
mechanical energy. Many pupils are fascinated by devices which
incorporate moving parts, where something can be seen to be
happening. The Gears assignments and the Basic Electricity
assignments form a link between static devices and the design,
construction, and use of devices involving motion.

In Assignment 1, pupils examine the properties of a number of
common gear systems. Pupils' diagrams of spur-gear systems need
consist only of circles in contact; the number of teeth on a
particular gear being written within the appropriate circle (e.g.
57T).

Assignment 2 introduces chain and belt drives. Pupils are asked to
compare these two systems with spur-gear systems.

Concepts of friction and mechanical efficiency are studied in Gears
Assignments 3 and 4. The former is illustrated by experiencing the
effort required to turn certain gear shafts, whilst the latter is
covered by making use of the six-speed Meccano electric motor and
gearbox. This versatile motor is used frequently in the course.
An investigation into its capabilities is, therefore, appropriate
at this stage.

Gears Assignment 4 includes the use of electrical measuring
instruments: the ammeter and the voltmeter. Unless the pupils have
some prior knowledge and experience in the use of meters, this
assignment should be deferred until after the Basic Electricity
Assignments. Gears Follow-up 4 may need further explanation for
less-able pupils.

GEARS ASSIGNMENT 1

For this programme, it is suggested that the class is divided into
five groups of three pupils, each group investigating, in turn, the
five different gear systems provided. These five systems demonstrate various ways of transmitting rotary motion and should be
constructed before the commencement of the lesson. Some construction notes are included, but these are intended only to give
guidance. Other arrangements may be found more satisfactory, or
different constructional material could be used, e.g. the mounting
frame could be made from Perspex, the axle holes being positioned
by using a Meccano strip as a template.

If the investigations are carried out carefully, and a full record
is made, pupils should experience little difficulty in drawing
conclusions which apply to all gear systems.

The Meccano range includes bevel and helical gears and, if these
are available, it is suggested that units using them are
constructed and shown to the class. However, these gears are
expensive and more difficult to use than the contrate and spur
gears.

Apparatus Required

Various pairs of Meccano gears can be selected to give whole number
ratios,

e.g. 25T and 50T
     19T and 38T or 57T or 95T or 133T
     15T and 60T

In the programme, particular gears are specified to simplify the
follow-up sheets; if these gears are not available, others may be
used provided the notes are modified accordingly.

With the simple system, little support is needed for the gear
shafts, but if improved bearings are required, as for example in
System 3, it is suggested that part number 62b (the double-arm
crank) be used for this purpose.

Construction of gear systems

SYSTEM 1: simple train of spur gears

Parts required	Part no.
one 19T gear	26
one 57T gear	27a
two axle rods, 50-75mm	
one flanged plate, 60 x 38mm	51
two collars	59
one washer	38

SYSTEM 2: simple train of spur gears with an idler

Parts required   Part no.
one flanged plate, 90 x 60mm   53
two 57T gears   27a
one 19T gear   26
three collars   59
two washers   38
two axle rods, 50-75mm
one axle rod, 25mm

SYSTEM 3: compound train of spur gears

Parts required	Part no.
one flanged plate, 90 x 60mm	53
two 60T gears	27d
two 15T gears	26c
three axle rods, 50-75mm	
three double-arm cranks	62b
1 washer	38
four collars	59

SYSTEM 4: spur gear and contrate gear

Parts required	Part no.
one flanged plate, 50-75mm	51
three trunnions	126
one double-arm crank	62b
three collars	59
one 50T contrate gear	28
one 25T pinion	25
one axle rod, 100mm	
one axle rod, 50mm	
one washer	38

(For diagram see overleaf.)

44

SYSTEM 5: worm gear and pinion

Parts required	Part no.
one flanged plate, 50 x 75mm	51
four trunnions	126
one 19T pinion	26
one worm	32
four collars	59
one axle rod, 100mm	
one axle rod, 75mm	
eight washers	38

(washers to be used as spacers <u>under</u> the trunnions.)

(For diagram see overleaf.)

Demonstrations

1 If Meccano bevel and helical gears are available, these systems
should be demonstrated.
2 Gear systems in everyday use can be demonstrated in the
following applications:
> spur gears (lathe screwcutting change gears; camshaft drive
> on some engines)
> worm and pinion (tennis-net tensioner)
> bevel gears (car rear-axle differential)
> helical gears (car distributor drive from camshaft; constant-
> mesh gearbox)

These demonstrations should lead to a general discussion on the use
of gear systems.

The following points might arise:

> quieter operation - advantages of helical gears,
> precision shaping of gears,
> critical positioning of gear shafts,
> lubrication,
> advantages of worm-and-pinion drives.

Buffer Experiments

1 If a car gearbox or back axle is available, pupils should
determine the ratios between input and output shafts. Similarly,

lathe screwcutting gear trains could be investigated. (Ensure the lathe is electrically isolated before the guard is removed.)

2 Devise a method of measuring the approximate forces needed to turn the input and output shafts.

Homework Questions

1 How many times must gear A be turned for gear B to turn once in the gear system shown below?

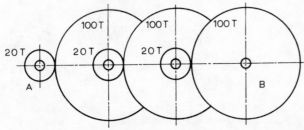

2 A car engine drives a shaft to which is fixed a gear with 20 teeth. A reduction in shaft speed of 3.5:1 is required (i.e. the engine turns 3.5 times to turn the gearbox output shaft once). How many teeth are required on the gearbox shaft gear?

3 Gears A and B rotate on shafts in fixed positions. Gear A can be rotated only in the direction shown; B, however, must have provision to be driven in either direction. Can you suggest a solution to this problem?

4 The diagram shows a rack and pinion (ensure that you have seen one of these before attempting the question). If the pinion rotates at 50 rev/min, how fast does the rack travel, and in which direction?

5   The motor in a electric clock runs at 300 rev/min. What gear
    ratios are required to drive (a) the second hand, (b) the
    minute hand, (c) the hour hand of the clock?

GEARS ASSIGNMENT 2

This programme deals with the transmission of rotary motion by
chain and belt systems. The investigations, again carried out in
small groups, are similar to those in Gears 1. It is suggested
that two of each type of system are constructed, since only three
models are used.

After examining various ways of transmitting rotary motion, pupils
should have gained sufficient knowledge to:

    select the most suitable transmission system for a given purpose;
    calculate the sizes of gears, pulleys, etc. required in a system.

This will enable them to solve, with confidence, the transmission
problems that they are likely to meet in future practical examples.

It is suggested that some classroom time be devoted to working
through a few typical problems, so that pupils are able to tackle
them in a methodical way.

Apparatus Required

Two of each of the following systems should be made; six units in
all. All systems are constructed in a similar way.

SYSTEM 1: Chain-and-sprocket system

Parts required	Part no.
one flanged plate, 140 x 60mm	52
one 25mm, 18T sprocket	96
one 50mm, 36T sprocket	95
two axle rods, 50mm	
two collars	59
one chain	94

SYSTEMS 2 AND 3: Pulley-and-belt system

Parts required	Part no.
one flanged plate, 140 x 60mm	52
one pulley, 25mm dia.	22
one pulley, 50mm dia.	20a
two axle rods, 50mm	
two collars	59
one driving band	186c
or spring cord and	58
coupling screw	58a

The bearings for the shafts may be improved by using two 62b double-arm crank as described in Gears 1.

Demonstrations

1 A bicycle chain-and-sprocket drive mechanism should be examined. The construction of the chain could be discussed. How is the chain tensioned and why? Why not use a belt or spur gears?

2 Various pulley systems should be examined in which flat, round, and vee-type belts are used,
   e.g. bench drilling-machine or lathe drive (vee belt),
        car engine-fan and generator drive (vee belt),
        sewing machine, either treadle or electrical (round belt),
        some workshop milling machines or older machines may use
        flat belts.

   Discuss the advantage of the vee belt over the flat belt. Stress the importance of tensioning the belt, and discuss the various ways of doing this.

3 If a car engine is available, discuss the method of driving the camshaft from the crankshaft, and compare this with the fan and generator drive. Why is a chain normally used for one drive and a belt for the other?

   This is an ideal time to discuss the new cogged belt used for driving some overhead camshafts.

Buffer Experiment

Calculate the overall gearing of a bicycle, i.e. the distance the bicycle moves forward for one revolution of the pedals. Pupils should then verify their answer by moving the pedals exactly one revolution and measuring the distance the bicycle moves forward.

Homework Questions

1 Make sketches of the following two diagrams:

indicate on each
a) the direction of rotation of each sprocket, and
b) the number of revolutions each gear makes if chain wheel A is turned three times.

2 What is the purpose of pulley A in the system shown below?

3 A bicycle pedal chain wheel has 48 teeth, and the rear sprocket has 18 teeth. If the pedal is rotated one complete revolution, how many times will the rear wheel rotate?

50

4   An electric motor fitted with a 100mm dia. pulley revolves at
    1500 rev/min. It is required to drive a circular saw at 2500
    rev/min. What size of pulley must be fitted to the saw spindle?

5   A bicycle has 560mm dia. wheels (including the tyres) and a
    pedal chain sprocket with 48 teeth. Three different sprockets
    are to be fitted to the rear wheel hub to provide three 'gears'.
    For each revolution of the front chain sprocket the bicycle
    should move distances of (a) 3.52m, (b) 5.28m, (c) 7.04m. How
    many teeth are needed on each of the three rear sprockets?

GEARS ASSIGNMENT 3

With pupils of above-average ability, this programme could be
carried out by means of group work, provided that five sets of
apparatus are available. However, with pupils of average and
below-average ability it is recommended that one set of apparatus
be used and that the teacher controls the experiments. Questioning
should ensure that the pupils understand the principles involved.

A certain amount of additional teaching may be necessary, depending
on the ability range and background knowledge of the pupils. For
instance, considerable time could be spent on defining the terms
'work' and 'energy'. The mathematics involved should be kept
simple, and perhaps left out altogether for the less able. In this
event, Gears Assignments 3 can be attempted by the pupils, but
Gears Follow-up 3 should be replaced by a simplified version.

Apparatus Required

SYSTEM 1

Parts required	Part no.
two flanged plates, 140 x 60mm	52
two angle girders, 320mm	1
four strips, 75mm	4
one 50T gear	27
one 25T gear	25
two axle rods, 75mm	
two anchoring springs	176
one hank of cord	40
one 1kg mass	
one spring-balance, reading to 1kg	

(For diagram see overleaf.)

SYSTEM 2: Nylon mounted axles

The list of parts required and the construction is identical to
that in system 1, except for the two axle rods. In addition, four
nylon bearings and eight 4 BA nuts are required, assembled as
shown.

Replace two 75mm axles with two axles as shown below.

If nylon is not available, a similar, well-lubricated brass bearing would provide greater efficiency than that provided by system 1.

Demonstrations

1 Illustrate the gear systems incorporated in overhead cranes etc.

2 Simple concepts of work and energy could be illustrated in the following way:

a) Discuss the meaning of energy in general terms: e.g. we eat food containing chemical energy, and within the body this energy is converted into
   i) heat energy, and
   ii) energy required to lift things or to perform other work.

b) Lift 1kg a vertical distance of 1 metre (say from the floor to a bench or low shelf). Establish the fact that energy from food has been used. Where has the energy gone?

Allow the mass to fall to the floor and to break safely a piece of wood etc. Establish that the energy was 'given' to the mass and that, when this fell, some energy was used in breaking the wood and the remainder was lost as heat. (Mention the heat generated when a hammer is used on metal.)

c) Lift 1kg a vertical distance of 2m. How much energy has been 'given' from chemical energy, and how much has the mass been 'given' in its new position?

d) Lift two 1kg masses (or preferably one 2kg mass) a vertical distance of 1m, 2m, etc. Establish that the energy transferred to the mass depends upon the vertical height raised and the mass.

Discuss the fact that 1kg lifted diagonally to a vertical height of 1m will do no more 'damage' in falling that 1kg lifted vertically, i.e. the energy given to the mass is the same.

Establish (using numerical values at first)

energy given to an object = force x distance (vertical)

Discuss units: N(force in newtons) x m(distance in metres)

N.B. The gravitational force acting on a mass of 1kg is about 10 newtons.

Hence energy given to an object = N m (newtons metres).

One newton metre (N m) is more commonly referred to as one joule (J).

e) Discuss the term 'work' as a measure of the amount of energy transferred from one form to another,

e.g. when 1kg (10 N) is lifted a vertical distance of 2m,

position (potential) energy given to the 1kg mass
= force x distance (vertical)
= 10 x 2 Nm
= 20 Nm
= 20 J

∴ amount of chemical energy transferred = 20 J
∴ work done in lifting the 1kg mass = 20 J

f) Several other simple calculations should be carried out.

Buffer Experiment

1 a) Repeat the assignment using a worm and pinion system.
Calculate its efficiency and compare it with the previous
systems used.
  b) Thoroughly lubricate the worm gear and pinion and the shaft
bearings. Is there an increase in efficiency?

2 Fix a small pulley to the shaft of the small gear. Attach the
cord to the pulley, instead of to the shaft, and repeat the
experiment. How do the results compare with those obtained in
the assignment? Try to account for any differences.

3 Attach the 1kg load to the cord on the small gear shaft and
apply the effort to the cord on the large gear shaft. Compare
your results with those in the assignment.

Homework Questions

1 If a simple two-gear system has a velocity ratio of, say, six,
and one gear has fifteen teeth, how many teeth has the other
gear?

2 A 100kg load attached by a cord to the shaft of a 40T gear wheel
driven by a worm is just raised by an effort of 100 N acting on
a cord around the other shaft. What is the efficiency of the
system if both shafts are of the same diameter?

3 In a similar gear system incorporating a 100T gear driven by a
25T gear, an effort of 2500 N is required to steadily raise a
load of 600kg. After the gears and shaft bearings have been well
lubricated, a 2000 N will just raise the same load. What is the
increase in efficiency of the system?

4 A machine raises a load of 180kg a distance of 2m. The effort,
a force of 240 N, moves 18m during the process. Calculate the
velocity ratio, mechanical advantage, and the efficiency at this
load.

GEARS ASSIGNMENT 4

As this investigation involves the use of both a voltmeter and an
ammeter, it is recommended that the Basic Electricity section is
completed before this programme is attempted.

Although pupils find the experiment well within their capabilities,
care must be taken to switch off the motor in good time, before the
load carrier reaches the Meccano frame. If fouling does occur, the
motor gearbox will probably be damaged. For this reason, the use
of the 3:1 gearbox ratio is not recommended, because the load is
then lifted too quickly.

This experiment can be developed further depending upon the ability and background knowledge of the pupils. Using each gear ratio in turn, the distance a load is lifted in a specific time can be recorded (keeping the voltage and current constant, as before). The work done in each case is calculated and comparisons made.

If the pupils have a sound knowledge of electricity, it might be possible to determine the overall efficiency of the system by calculating the electrical energy used by the motor and the work done by the motor in lifting the load.

Apparatus Required
LIFTING DEVICE (FIVE REQUIRED)

Parts required	Part no.
two angle girders, 320mm	1
one angle girder, 240mm	1a
two flanged plates, 90 x 60mm	53
two flanged plates, 60 x 38mm	51
two strips, 60mm	5
four corner brackets	133
one axle rod, 130mm	
one flexible coupling	175
two couplings	63
one anchoring spring	176
one hank of cord	40
one six-speed electric motor	

Other items required:
ten weights to stand on platform to provide stability (two per group)
ten loads (1kg) consisting of ten 100g masses (two loads per group)
five loads (100g) consisting of ten 10g masses (one load per group)

```
voltmeters reading 0-10V
ammeters reading 0-1A
12V d.c. power supplies
leads with 4mm plugs
```

Demonstrations

1 A possible demonstration for the more able pupils is suggested
under 'Buffer experiments'.

2 Demonstrate the effect on the current consumption of the motor,
and on lifting speed, when the layers of cord pile one on top
of another. Establish that the effect is similar to changing
the motor to a lower gear ratio.

3 Demonstrate the 3:1 ratio to show that the lifting speed is
excessive, warning that damage can occur to the motor if it is
not stopped in time. Pupils are instructed not to use the 3:1
ratio.

4 Adjust the Meccano motor to engage the 6:1 ratio. Lift a 1kg
load and note the voltage and current. Switch off the supply
(holding the load) and show that, when the load is released,
electrical energy is generated as indicated by the voltmeter.
This emphasises that the electrical energy produces mechanical
(potential) energy which can be used to produce electrical
energy again. Light a 12V, 2.2W bulb, by placing a lamp indicator unit in the circuit, in addition to showing a meter
reading.
(Note: To obtain positive voltmeter readings when the motor acts
as a generator, the reversing switch on the motor must be
changed over.)

load lifted

12V, 2·2W

load falling

change-over
reversing switch

Buffer Experiments

1 Repeat the assignment, this time measuring the vertical distance
that the load is lifted in some specific time.

Calculate and compare the work done by the motor when alternative gear atios are engaged. (i.e. compare the work done in a

given time - power or rate of working).

2 The overall efficiency of the system can be investigated by the
   whole group (if they are of above average ability) or covered
   by demonstration. Set up the apparatus as before (assignment
   4). Choose a gear ratio and a suitable load (F newtons).

   Record:
   a) the time (t) in seconds taken for the load to be lifted
      through a given distance (l) in metres,
   b) the ammeter reading (I),
   c) the voltmeter reading (V).

   Calculation:
   Rate of consumption of electrical energy (i.e. power supplied to
   motor) = VI joules/second
   ∴ energy supplied to the motor (in time t) = VIt joules (or
   newton metres)

   Work carried out by the machine (in time t) = force x distance
   (vertical) = F x l

   $$\text{Efficiency} = \frac{\text{useful work carried out by machine}}{\text{total energy put into machine}}$$

   $$= \frac{F \times l}{VIt} \times 100\%$$

Homework Questions

1 Explain why it is virtually impossible for a motor car to move
   off, from rest, in top gear.

2 The diagram shows a device
   for lifting water from a
   well. If the bucket and
   water exert a force of
   200 N what is the least
   possible force needed to
   turn the handle? If the
   rope coils were to pile on
   top of each other, what
   effect would this have on
   the force needed to turn
   the handle?

3 The gears in the gearbox of the electric motor you have used are
   most easily damaged through overloading when the 60:1 ratio is
   used. Explain why this is so.

Basic electricity

This section of the course is included to give pupils sufficient background knowledge of electricity to enable them to tackle the Electrical Switching assignments which follow. They should have a working knowledge of current, voltage, resistance, the use of the voltmeter and ammeter, and be familiar with common electrical symbols. Three programmes are included, though some teachers may wish to omit Electricity 3, which deals with Ohm's law. During the second year of the course, applications of Ohm's Law are dealt with more fully in the Electronics: resistance assignments.

Some teachers may be tempted to devise further programmes for this section of the course, but it is recommended that they should first cover the complete course at least once, in order to fully appreciate the purpose of the Electricity programmes and the manner in which they link with others.

BASIC ELECTRICITY ASSIGNMENT 1

Firstly a number of basic electrical symbols are introduced. Perhaps the most important of these, at this stage, is the switch symbol. Emphasis should be placed on the use of a 'solid' circle to represent the pole of a switch and the 'open' circle to represent contacts. Later programmes include fairly complex switching-circuit diagrams and, unless the poles are clearly marked, the circuits are difficult to follow.

The pupils are asked to connect a single bulb to a single cell and a switch, and to observe the effect when the switch is closed. For this experiment a 1.5V cell should be used in conjunction with a 1.5V lamp. Cell-carrier units are available which house six U2-type cells, the ends of the cells being connected independently to 4mm sockets. This unit facilitates the connection of cells in series and parallel.

Having seen the bulb illuminated with the cell one way round, the pupils are then asked to reverse the cell. An ammeter is then used (1A full-scale deflection, approximately) to find the current taken by a single lamp run at its normal intensity When two, then three, cells are connected in series with one lamp, it is advisable to suggest that the tests should be as short in duration as possible, otherwise bulb filaments are likely to 'blow'. These experiments are important since they give the pupils an insight into the relationship between voltage and current and the effect of fitting cells in series.

Parallel circuits are investigated using lamps connected in parallel. Pupils should learn from this that currents can divide and that currents can be measured in a circuit by fitting an ammeter anywhere in it. In effect they simply 'cut' a lead and insert the meter. Should the resistance of the meter cause a lamp brightness to diminish, then a fruitful discussion on the 'resistance' of ammeters could follow. The currents in a parallel circuit are compared with those in a series circuit. Brighter pupils may suggest that the lower brightness of series bulbs is due to the increased circuit resistance.

Apparatus Required (15 pupils, 5 groups of 3)

cells: three per group (1.5V) in a suitable housing, e.g. a cell-carrier unit fitted with 4mm output sockets

lamps: four per group (1.5V, 0.25A)

switches: one per group, single pole on-off. The double-pole, double-throw toggle switch unit, or the S.P.D.T. push-button switch could be used

ammeters: one per group, approximately 1 ampere full-scale deflection

leads: nine per group (fitted with stackable 4mm plugs)

Demonstrations

A number of different types of cell, and ammeters with different scale deflections, could be demonstrated.

Buffer Experiments

1 If enough lamps and holders are available, try more than two lamps in series and in parallel.

2 Offer a universal meter, to replace the ammeter in the circuits, and try the effect of using different ranges. Ask the pupils to decide whether a large or small deflection of the pointer gives the most accurate value for the currents flowing.

3 Provide a relay, and ask the pupils to discover at what current the relay energises.

4 Provide a high-current solenoid. Ask the pupils to connect it across eight U2-type cells in series, and compare the results with the effect when the solenoid is connected across a car battery.

Homework Questions

1 Draw a circuit diagram to show how you would connect two 6V lamps to a battery giving 12V so that each will light normally. How much current would you expect to be drawn from the battery, compared with that drawn when one of the lamps is used?

2 Draw a circuit diagram to show how you would connect two 12V motors in series with a 12V battery.
What can you say about the speed of each motor, compared with the speed of a single 12V motor connected to a 12V battery?

3 Would you expect motor-car lamps to be connected in series or parallel? Show how you would connect an ammeter into a motor-car circuit in such a way that it would register the current taken by any combination of lamps.

4 Draw a circuit diagram containing one on-off switch, two ammeters, two 6V lamps, two motors, and a 6V battery. The lamps should glow less brightly than normally. One ammeter should read the current taken by one motor and the other the total current in the circuit. The switch in its 'off' position should prevent any current being taken from the battery.

BASIC ELECTRICITY ASSIGNMENT 2

This programme introduces the voltmeter as a means of measuring electrical 'force'. Cells can be fitted in parallel using a cell carrier. Pupils will discover, at a later date, that not all power supplies are capable of providing large currents.

Basic Electricity Follow-up 2 raises the question of the resistance of a circuit, and it is intended that at this stage the teacher should discuss resistance in more general terms with his pupils. Should any ideas be put forward, then the class could devise experiments to test them.

Apparatus Required (15 pupils, 5 groups of 3)

cells: two per group (1.5V), in suitable carrier

lamps: one per group

switches: one per group, single-pole on-off

ammeters: one per group, approximately 1 ampere full-scale deflection

voltmeters: one per group, approximately 5 volts full-scale deflection accumulator: 12V motor-car lead-acid battery

Demonstration

1 Allow pupils to see and examine a number of voltmeters with different ranges. Demonstrate a universal meter such as the Avometer. If appropriate, mention alternating current, and also that the Avometer is one of the types of meter which will measure both a.c. and d.c.

2 Demonstrate the low internal resistance of a motor-car battery - ensure it is well charged - by shorting out the negative and positive terminals with one strand of a length of multi-stranded insulated wire. Repeat the procedure using eight U2-type cells in series, and compare the results.

Buffer Experiments

1 Use a universal meter to replace the voltmeter and ammeter.

2 Replace the lamps with an electric motor and measure the current flowing in the motor with differing supply voltages. Find a relationship between motor speed and supply voltage.

3 Investigate the current carried by the motor under differing load conditions. The motor can be loaded by trying to stop the motor shaft turning by gripping with the fingers - this is not recommended on the 60:1 ratio, as damage to the gearbox may result.

Homework Questions

1 If you were Chief Engineer at a power station feeding only one small town, how would you prevent damage to the generators if the current consumed by customers was increasing to a dangerous level? Suggest three different methods.

2 Two 6V lamps with a voltmeter across each are connected in series with a 12V battery. Each lamp glows with the same brightness. Suddenly one lamp becomes very dim and the reading on its voltmeter falls. The other lamp immediately becomes very bright and its voltmeter reading increases. Suggest what could have happened to give this effect.

3 A machine requires a 12V supply, and it consumes a large current. You have eighteen cells each of 2V. Show how you would connect the cells to the machine so that it would run normally for the longest time possible.

BASIC ELECTRICITY ASSIGNMENT 3

This programme could be attempted by the brighter pupils, who will benefit by knowing the relationship between voltage, current, and resistance. Then the knowledge should be consolidated by calculating relay currents and resistances when relays are used in switching circuits.

Apparatus Required (15 pupils, 5 groups of 3)

Variable voltage supplies: one per group. The Universal Labpack produced by Radford Laboratory Instruments Ltd is recommended. This supply will provide an a.c. or d.c. output from 0 to 25V at 8A maximum in 0.2V steps.

Resistance wire: a reel of resistance wire such as Eureka 26 s.w.g.

Demonstrations

If variable-voltage supply units are in short supply, some teachers may wish to demonstrate this programme.

Buffer Experiments

1 Graph the results of one of the experiments, plotting voltage against current. Repeat the experiment with a filament lamp, to demonstrate the increase in resistance of the filament at a high temperature.

2 Graph the voltage/current relationship for a semiconductor diode.

Homework Questions

1 If in the circuit shown below the voltmeter reads 6V and the ammeter 2A, what is the effective motor resistance?

2 The heating element in a small electric furnace has a resistance of 50 ohms. What current flows in the element when it is connected to the 250V mains?

3   The filament in a lamp is most likely to 'burn out' when it is
    first switched on. Why do you think this is so?

4   If in the circuit shown below A_1 reads 1 ampere, A_2 reads 2
    amperes, A_3 reads 3 amperes, and the voltmeter reads 6V,

    a) which lamp will give out the most light?
    b) which lamp has the lowest filament resistance?
    c) what current is taken from the battery?
    d) what is the resistance of the filament of L_1?
    e) what is the resistance of the filament of L_2?
    f) what is the resistance of the filament of L_3?

Electrical switching

Pupils attempting this section of the course should have some knowledge of the fundamental principles of electricity. It is important that they have been introduced to basic ideas of voltage, current, and resistance and have measured voltages and currents. They should also have a knowledge of the common electrical symbols, such as those for the cell, battery, resistor, switch, and lamp, and should be able to draw simple circuits. Ideally, the Basic-electricity assignments, which cover these points will have been attempted before beginning the Electrical-switching assignments.

The Electrical-switching assignments are intended to introduce pupils to methods of electrical control and to some of the more important sensing devices used in control systems. The electro-magnetic relay is used frequently, and pupils become familiar with relatively complex switching circuitry involving delays, flip-flops (bistables), and clocks (oscillators). The operation of a relay is easily understood by the average pupil. Experience has shown that many pupils who have only a modest knowledge of magnetism and electricity can reason how the device operates, following brief examination. What is not so easily grasped is the relationship between the applied voltage, the resistance, the current, and the number of turns on the coil for a given relay. When pupils have used a number of different relays in a variety of situations, they will more easily appreciate these factors and consider them when designing circuitry for major project work later in the course. Whenever appropriate, therefore, we should encourage pupils to think about relay circuitry design in terms of the relay they are using at a particular time.

The Electrical-switching assignments can be summarised as follows:

Assignment 1: A vehicle is designed to meet a given specification. Here the pupils apply their knowledge of structures and gearing to produce a rigid vehicle moving at a specific speed.

Assignment 2: The use of a two-pole, two-way switch unit is investigated by pupils to discover which pairs of sockets are connected in the two possible positions of the switch toggle. Pupils use switch units to stop, start, and reverse the vehicle.

Assignment 3: Pupils use reed-switch and microswitch sensors to indicate when the vehicle strikes an obstruction.

Assignment 4: The relay is introduced through the two-pole, two-way relay unit. Pupils investigate the switching in a similar manner to that used in the switch-unit investigations. They are asked to design and assemble a circuit consisting of a reed-switch and relay to make the vehicle reverse when it strikes an obstruction.

Assignment 5: Using a microswitch and relay, pupils set up a circuit which will enable their vehicle to reverse when it strikes an obstruction. A capacitor is fitted across the relay coil to produce a time delay before the relay de-energises. Using a number of different capacitor values, pupils discover an approximate relationship between delay time and capacitance.

Assignment 6: Here the bistable principle is introduced. Pupils investigate a relay-bistable unit and then use it to cause their vehicle to reverse when it strikes an obstruction, and to continue reversing until a second obstruction is encountered.

Assignment 7: Pupils now investigate the use of the light-dependent resistor (photocell). Using the cell and a relay, pupils are asked to make their vehicle stop when it breaks a beam of light.

Assignment 8: Using a photocell and one relay, pupils are asked to design and test a circuit which will cause their vehicle to oscillate in and out of a light beam. Three alternative values of capacitor are fitted across the relay coil, and pupils observe the effect in each case.

Assignment 9: Pupils again attempt to make their vehicle reverse out of a beam of light, but a second relay is incorporated. The operation of this second relay is delayed.

Assignment 10: Using a relay-bistable unit and two photocell units, a vehicle is made to oscillate between two beams of light.

Note: It is recommended that assignments 9 and 10 become teacher demonstrations for all but the most able children. Some teachers may also wish to demonstrate assignment 8.

For the first Electrical-switching assignments, it is perhaps advisable to allow pupils to record their circuits simply as switch-unit diagrams. As soon as it is expedient, however, encourage the drawing of electrical circuit diagrams alongside, and eventually discourage the use of any type of diagram which is not conventional.

British Standards suggest the following means of showing wires which are electrically connected and those which are not.

A,B,C connected   A and B not connected

The following convention is sometimes used, but is now out of date and should be discontinued.

A,B,C connected   A and B not connected

ELECTRICAL-SWITCHING ASSIGNMENT 1

Using their knowledge of structures and gear systems, pupils produce a design, in their notebooks, for a vehicle which will run at 1.1 m/min, given that the wheels are 35mm diameter and the motor output-shaft speed is 200 rev/min. No construction is attempted at this time. Encourage pupils to draw sketches of a number of possible vehicle designs (at least three) and to select the best solution, giving reasons. The chosen solution should be drawn fully, including measurements. When constructed, the vehicle should be large enough to carry control equipment such as a relay unit and capacitor or a bistable unit. It is advisable, therefore, to suggest to pupils that the completed vehicle should be no smaller than, say, 25cm long and 12cm wide.

When all have completed the design stage, it may be desirable to have a general discussion. Also, make a typical calculation on the blackboard to emphasise that calculations should be recorded in a clear and logical manner. Before any construction can be attempted pupils must know:

a)   the actual output-shaft speed, using a given gear ratio;
b)   what Meccano gears are available.

Pupils are asked to think of a method of finding the motor speed. Most will no doubt use the motor on the 60:1 ratio and count the number of revolutions in a given time, using a marker on the motor shaft. For this they will require a stop watch or stop clock. Other possibilities should be considered and, when all methods have been tried, the teacher should show that the shaft speed of a high-speed motor can be measured using a photocell and an electro-magnetic counter (see Electrical-switching follow-up 1). The maximum speed of operation of an electromagnetic counter is about 10 pulses per second, which corresponds to a motor speed of 600 rev/min. For higher speeds the electromagnetic counter can be replaced by an electronic counter. The teacher may wish to demonstrate some of the other possible methods.

When pupils have collected together the parts for their vehicles, they may have wheels and gears of slightly different sizes from those used in their calculations. On the basis of their new information, (motor speed, wheel size, and gears) they should recalculate the theoretical vehicle speed. The vehicle should then be constructed and tested over a suitable distance.

The teacher should check each vehicle for rigidity and reliability, once completed, since it will be used throughout the Electrical-switching assignment programmes. Checks should be made especially on motor-mounting methods, to ensure correct meshing of gears under all reasonable load conditions.

Apparatus Required (15 pupils, 5 groups of 3)

assorted Meccano parts (these must include a sufficient number of wheels with rubber tyres to prevent slipping), spur gears, worm gears and axles

five stop watches or stop clocks

five 1 metre rules

chalk - for marking motor shafts and for marking out the start and finish of a test track.

Demonstrations

1 Select a gear ratio which makes it impossible to count the rotations of the output shaft. Show that such speeds can be determined using an electromagnetic counter and a photocell.

SUITABLE COUNTER

The counter should ideally operate at about 12 V or less. With the motor running and the disc rotating, adjust the battery voltage (use a variable d.c. supply) until the counter works correctly. Avoid allowing light to strike the cell when the motor is stationary, otherwise damage to the cell may result.

LIGHT SOURCE AND PHOTOCELL

Use a light-source unit (12 V, 2.2 W) and a photocell unit.

DISC AND BUSH

62b

12 mm dia hole

hardboard disc

100 mm dia disc

2 To count the rotations of a high-speed motor shaft, an electronic counter (e.g. a decade scaler) can be used.

photocell

R

DECADE SCALER

Input

3 Demonstrate any other methods of determining motor-shaft speeds, e.g. using a stroboscope.

Buffer Experiments

1 Arrange for the vehicle to ascend an incline. Find the maximum angle of incline which the vehicle will travel up. Compare the result with other vehicles.

2 Arrange for the vehicle to ascend an incline. Add some extra weight and try again. What conclusions can be drawn? Repeat for other weights.

Homework Questions

1   A vehicle covers 2.5m in 12 seconds. What is the average speed of the vehicle? How far will the vehicle travel in one minute at this speed?

2   A vehicle with 50mm diameter wheels travels 4m in 3 seconds. If the wheels are reduced to 40mm diameter, what speed would you expect the vehicle to have?

3   When a vehicle travels over level ground, energy (electrical or chemical from petrol etc.) is consumed by the motor. What happens to this energy? If the vehicle climbs an incline, what happens to energy put into the motor?

4   Describe a method of finding the speed of rotation of a motor shaft which is too fast to measure by counting directly yourself.

5   Which of the following would <u>not</u> affect the speed of your vehicle:

   a) the radius of the driving wheels?
   b) the voltage supplied to the motor?
   c) the gear ratio?
   d) the axle diameter?
   e) the diameter of the wheels which are not driven?

ELECTRICAL-SWITCHING ASSIGNMENT 2

This is the first of several assignments concerned with the various types of switches, e.g. manual switch, microswitch, reed-switch, photocell, relay, etc. (Note that in Electrical-switching Assignment 7 the photocell is first introduced as a variable resistor but, in conjunction with a relay, is used by the pupils as a light-operated switch.) Before attempting Electrical-switching Assignment 2, the most we can assume is that pupils are aware of the single pole on-off switch.

single-pole on-off

In this assignment we introduce switches with several poles and several 'ways'. One could draw several types on the blackboard and trust that the pupils develop a useful insight into switches in general; however, this method will not have the same impact as offering a new type of switch for them to investigate.

Pupils are given a two-way, two-pole (two-pole change-over) manual switch unit, and are asked to discover which pairs of sockets are 'joined together' with the switch in the 'up' and then in the 'down' position. In effect we are calling on the pupils' knowledge of on-off switches and showing that there are four pairs of sockets which become on-off switches. The 'short-circuit' detector used is the vehicle motor in series with a 12 volt supply. This is far more meaningful at this stage than offering the ohmmeter as a means of detecting short-circuits. Obviously a lamp indicator unit could be used.

Alternative short-circuit detector

Having determined which pairs of sockets became short-circuited, pupils are asked to use the switch to isolate the motor completely from the supply, anticipating the following:

or

If the motor leads are in the position of the supply leads, and vice versa, the solution is just as acceptable.

At this stage the teacher should discuss two important points relating to mains switches.

a) By convention, a manual switch in the 'up' position should indicate an 'off' condition and in the 'down' position an 'on' condition (except on stairways). Unfortunate accidents can occur if this convention is reversed. (It is desirable, but not always possible, to switch off the entire mains supply in a building.)

b) Again for safety, mains equipment should be completely isolated from the supply by using a two-pole on-off switch, though electrically a single pole on-off is equally effective.

71

Reversing circuits are introduced by asking pupils to make their vehicle go in one direction with the switch in the up position and to reverse in the switch 'down' position. Although this appears to be a large step, experience has shown that the average pupils can solve the problem relatively quickly. This shows the wisdom of introducing the manual switch box in the manner suggested, thereby giving pupils complete insight into the two-pole, two-way switch. In order to assist pupils, but mainly to prevent excessive short-circuiting of the supply, pupils are instructed to place the motor leads into the yellow sockets (the switch poles). If difficulty is encountered, refer pupils to Electrical-switching Assignment 2 (section 3).

Finally, pupils are asked to make use of a second manual switch unit so that they can make their vehicle stop - in addition to moving forwards and reversing. The obvious solution is to use the second unit to break a motor supply lead. It is interesting to note, however, that one or two groups frequently offer the solution below.

wired as two separate one-pole, two-way switches

In effect this solution prevents the two switches in a single switch unit from acting together, i.e. they have removed the 'ganging'. Electrical-switching Follow-up 2 suggests that those who have not tried this method should do so. Later, in logic circuitry, pupils will meet this arrangement again in the form of a useful logic 'gate'.

Electrical-switching Follow-up 2 shows switches with differing poles and ways. These should be recorded for future reference. Note that shaded circles are used for 'pole' and open circles for 'ways'.

normally-closed contact

normally-open contact

pole

Apparatus Required (15 pupils, 5 groups of 3)

five vehicles fitted with a motor (made in Assignment 1)

ten manual switch units (two-pole, two-way)

stackable 4mm plug leads - assorted lengths

five power supplies - 12 V d.c. 5A - with safety fuse or trip

Demonstrations

a) Discuss mains isolation using two-pole on-off switches.

b) Show room-lighting switches as one-pole on-off. Discuss the danger of removing faulty lamps (e.g. broken glass) if neutral is switched rather than live.

c) Discuss 'earthing' of electrical appliances for safety - if the 'live' side of the mains shorts to an 'earthed' metal case, the fuse blows; if the metal case is not earthed, it becomes 'live'.

d) Establish the fact that one can place a switch in either the positive or negative lead from a battery, but that the mains 'live' lead should be switched.

e) Show how to wire up a mains plug.

f) Demonstrate several types of switches, including wafer switches, with assorted poles and ways.

Buffer Experiments

1 Wire up a reversing circuit which also provides for on-off switching using two separate one-pole, two-way switches, but replace the motor with a lamp unit. In what way are the results using a lamp different from those obtained when a motor is used? Tabulate your motor and lamp results, and try to explain the differences.

2 Set up your circuit as in 1 and, using a lamp indicator, check that the lamp is on or off in the switch positions shown in your table. Now rewire the circuit such that the results are the reverse of those in your table.

Homework Questions

1 On a stairway there are usually two switches, one at the top and one at the bottom of the stairs. You will have noticed that, unlike any other switch in your house, you can sometimes

put the stairway light 'on' by putting one of the switches up,
but at other times the same switch must be down. Establish
this on your stairway lighting at home, then show how you can
do the same thing using a 12 volt supply, a 12 volt lamp unit,
and two manual switch units.

2   Draw a diagram to show how you could use only two switches in a
circuit with three lamps such that one, two, or three lamps can
be switched on.

3   What kind of switch (i.e. one-pole on-off; two-pole, two-way;
etc.) should be used to:

   a) operate a living-room light?
   b) operate a light on a stairway?
   c) switch an electric cooker on and off?
   d) switch a battery portable radio on and off?

4   Draw an electrical circuit diagram of this arrangement:

Describe what happens when

a) the switch is 'up',
b) the switch is 'down'.

5   What is the purpose of this circuit?
Draw an electrical circuit diagram of the arrangement.

This assignment introduces pupils to the microswitch and the reed-
switch. A microswitch is required which is robust, will operate at
low forces, and is of the single-pole, change-over type. The switch
contacts are connected to three 4mm sockets, to enable connections
to be made quickly. The reed-switch should have heavy-current
contacts and be of the single-pole, on-off, normally-open type. The
reed-switch is fragile and must be protected against mechanical
damage. The 4mm sockets are connected to the switch contacts to
facilitate quick assembly.

Should a heavy current be passed in the reed-switch contacts,
brought about by shorting out the supply with the switch, welding
of the contacts is likely to occur, preventing their opening when
the magnetising force is removed. Usually the fault can be cleared
by giving a sharp tap with a small screwdriver. Again, large
capacitors should not be discharged or charged rapidly through
reed-switch contacts, since welding will occur. When pupils use a
capacitor/relay delay in Electrical-switching Assignment 5, a microswitch with heavier contacts is used, rather than a reed-switch.
The microswitch contacts are able to carry the capacitor charging
current, which can be very large at the instant of switch closure.

Pupils are offered a microswitch in Electrical-switching Assignment
3(1) and are asked to test it to discover the type of switch used.
It is anticipated that they will use similar tests to those used
for the manual switch unit. The microswitch is attached to the
vehicle, and no difficulty should be experienced in making the
vehicle motor stop when an obstruction operates the switch. When
pupils draw this simple circuit diagram, it should be a conventional
electrical circuit. To indicate a microswitch, a suitable method
is as follows:

microswitch

When it is convenient, introduce the use of the terms 'normally-open
contact' - NO - and 'normally-closed contact' - NC. In any switch
which is biased one way (e.g. a microswitch or a relay), circuit
diagrams should be drawn showing the switch in the unoperated
position, as follows:

12 V

microswitch shown in
unoperated condition, i.e.
before vehicle strikes
obstruction

In the case of a relay, the unoperated condition is when the coil does not pass a current.

Later, pupils examine a reed-switch. Each group should also be given two bar magnets. When the magnet approaches a reed-switch, a 'click' is quite audible as the contacts close. Before fitting the reed-switch to the vehicle, pupils should ascertain that it is a single pole, on-off switch. Having easily arranged for a lamp to be illuminated, pupils will try to make the vehicle move with the reed-switch in series with the supply and will be unsuccessful unless a magnet is placed alongside the reed. It is important to know that this on-off switch is 'normally-open', and the teacher should discuss this with each group as he observes them at work.

In order to make the vehicle stop when it approaches a magnet on an obstruction, the two magnets must be orientated such that they attract. The vehicle should stop at a short distance from the obstruction. All groups should be able to solve this problem after a hesitant start, but they will find that the reed biasing magnet position is very critical. It is intended that pupils should not be entirely satisfied with this arrangement, since the next assignment introduces a relay method which is far more reliable.

Apparatus Required

five microswitch units

five reed-switch units

ten strong bar magnets - poles marked (25-50mm long)

five vehicles - constructed in Electrical-switching Assignment 1
    stackable 4mm plug leads - assorted lengths

five power supplies - 12 V d.c., 5 A - with safety fuse or trip

five lamp indicator units

five suitable obstructions - wooden blocks etc.

Demonstrations

1   Discuss the meaning of 'normally-open' and 'normally-closed'
    contacts. Show a dismantled microswitch to locate the biasing
    spring.

2   Show a selection of microswitches. Demonstrate that some
    require larger forces than others, and that the type of switch
    (poles and ways) can vary.

3   Show a selection of reed-switches. Discuss why smaller types
    have smaller contacts and cannot pass large currents. If
    possible, demonstrate a single-pole change-over type (RS
    Components type 13-RSR, or similar). Set up suitable circuits
    to demonstrate these.

4   Demonstrate the use of a coil to provide a magnetic field for
    the reed (RS Components reed coil type 1).

    e.g.

5   Fit a reed-switch to a device such as a lathe bed. Fit a bar
    magnet to the carriage. Arrange for a lamp to illuminate when
    the magnet approaches the reed. Discuss whether the reed used
    as a 'limit switch' would be suitable to give a warning to the
    operator.

Buffer Experiments

Wire up your vehicle motor to a manual switch unit so that you can
make the vehicle move forward or reverse. Fit a microswitch to
each end of your vehicle. Somewhere on the vehicle fit a lamp
indicator unit. Arrange for the lamp to be illuminated when the

vehicle strikes an obstruction and, each time it illuminates, reverse the motor with the switch box. Draw your circuit before actual wiring up.

Homework Questions

1 Manual push-button on-off switches are available from certain manufacturers. The button is maintained in the up position by a spring, and the switch is operated by pushing against it. These switches are 'normally-open' or 'normally-closed' Imagine you manufacture these two types of switch and write a brief explanation of each.

2 Describe what happens in the circuit below if one or both of the magnets A and B are placed next to the change-over reed-switches (A and B). Assume that in the diagram the magnets are too far away from the reed-switches to operate the contacts.

3 The intention with the circuit below is for the lamp L to be switched off when a magnet is placed near to the reed-switch, provided that switch S is closed.

a) Is the lamp switched off?
b) Why is the circuit not a good one?
c) Redraw the circuit to show your modifications.

4   The diagram shows the type of microswitch which is intended to operate when a force F is applied at the end of the rigid bar as shown. Unfortunately, F is too small to operate the switch and cannot be made larger.

a)   What could you do to enable the force F to operate the switch reliably?

b)   The force F required to just operate the switch is 0.1N. The distance of the pivot from A is 20mm and the distance from the pivot to F is 100mm. What force applied directly on the plunger A would just operate the microswitch?

5   You wish to use a microswitch method to switch on a d.c. electric motor requiring a starting current of 3A. Unfortunately, although you have several identical microswitches, the contact current rating of each is 1 A d.c. maximum. How would you solve the problem?

ELECTRICAL-SWITCHING ASSIGNMENT 4

One of the aims of the Control Technology course is to encourage inventiveness. This is possible only if there are problems to solve and the materials with which to solve them. Electrical-switching Assignment 5 brings the pupils' first real acquaintance with the electromagnetic relay. This important control device is extremely versatile and can be used in a wide range of applications. The pupils meet several useful relay circuits in the basic course, and teachers will no doubt find that the more able ones will suggest other configurations to solve individual problems.

The manual switch unit was introduced by testing to find out which pairs of sockets became shorted out when the switch was operated. The relay is examined and pupils soon recognise that the two units are similar. Pupils are instructed to connect a 12 volt supply across the green sockets (relay-coil terminations) and to note the

effect by observing the relay operation. This is to establish that
the relay 'changes over'. If pupils have not met relays previously,
then this is the time to demonstrate several types, and to discuss
the principle of operation. Having completed their initial tests,
pupils should be left in no doubt that they are now dealing with a
two-pole, two-way, coil-operated switch.

The relay is used to control the vehicle and, in the first instance,
is employed to <u>invert</u> the switch function in the reed-switch unit.
Being normally-open, a reed-switch will not, unless biased with a
magnet, allow a vehicle motor to run. By putting the reed-switch
in series with the relay coil, the relay can act as an 'inverter'
or 'buffer' as shown.

inverter circuit

The reed-switch is normally-open and remains open until it is in
close proximity to a magnet. The motor is connected to a pair of
normally-closed contacts in series with the supply, and therefore
runs. When the reed-switch closes, due to the proximity of the
magnet, the relay energises and disconnects the supply to the motor.

Note that the only relay contacts required are one-pole on-off, the
second set of contacts being left disconnected in this case.

buffer circuit

If the relay contacts used are normally-open, as shown, the circuit
is electrically analogous to a reed-switch alone, and a magnet is
required to start the motor.

80

An advantage of this relay circuit is that the motor current is
carried by the relay contacts and not by the reed contacts. The
latter, therefore, carry only the small relay-coil current. The
maximum current permissible with most reed contacts is quite small
(less than 1A in general), whereas relay contacts can switch
several amperes. Experience has shown that for reliable inter-
mittent use the maximum d.c. current is in the region of 0.5
amperes for the reed-switch suggested (7RSR). This is the approximate starting current for a reasonably loaded Meccano motor. It
is therefore permissible to switch the motor current by means of
a reed-switch unit. If a larger motor were to be used, or a reed-
switch with a lower contact-current rating, then a relay buffer
would be essential.

Pupils should be made aware of these two uses of a relay at the
earliest opportunity, and, if the teacher thinks it appropriate at
this stage, he should now discuss the two applications. Note that
the terms 'buffer' and 'inverter' are not mentioned in the
Electrical-switching assignments, but pupils should be made
familiar with them.

The final investigation of Electrical-switching Assignment 4 is
concerned with finding a way of making the vehicle reverse away
from an obstruction fitted with a magnet. Pupils should find little
difficulty in wiring up a reversing circuit to the relay contacts,
and should succeed in making the vehicle reverse. Unfortunately,
as soon as the reed-switch is no longer influenced by the magnet
on the obstruction, the vehicle again reverses towards it. The
sequence repeats itself and the vehicle 'oscillates'.

Apparatus Required (15 pupils, 5 groups of 3)

five reed switch units

five two-pole change-over relay units

stackable 4mm plug leads - assorted lengths

five vehicles fitted with motors - made in Electrical-switching
Assignment 1

five power supplies - 12 V d.c., 5 A - with safety fuse or trip

Demonstrations

1   Demonstrate the relay functioning as a 'buffer' and as an
    'inverter'.

2   Demonstrate the operation of various relays, showing different
    sizes of coils and different types of contacts. Some Post
    Office types are particularly suitable for discussing the
    principle of operation.

3   Demonstrate and discuss the uniselector principle and applica-
    tions (see following notes).

4   Demonstrate the operation of an electromagnetic counter, and
    discuss its similarity to a relay.

Buffer Experiments

1   Connect up the relay unit in order to make the vehicle motor
    reverse when the relay is energised. Replace the reed-switch
    unit by a microswitch unit. Compare the results obtained when
    the microswitch strikes an obstruction with those using a reed-
    switch. Try to account for any differences in vehicle opera-
    tion.

2   It is possible to make a vehicle reverse away from an obstruc-
    tion, and continue reversing, by wiring up the relay in such a
    way that once it energises it remains so until the supply is
    switched off. Attempt to set up such a circuit, and draw it in
    your notebook.

Homework Questions

1   Draw an electrical
    circuit diagram
    for the arrange-
    ment shown oppo-
    site, and describe
    what happens when
    switch A is opened
    and closed.

2   Describe what is likely to happen in the circuit below, when
     the switch S is opened and closed.

3   Draw an electrical circuit diagram of a device which will enable
     a motor to run forwards, and reverse when an on-off switch is
     operated. When the motor runs forwards, a lamp (call it L_1)
     should illuminate; and when it reverses, a second lamp (L_2)
     should illuminate and L_1 should go out.

4   A motor, which operates from the mains 250V a.c. supply, is
     situated about 500m from a building. It must be possible to
     switch the motor on and off from the building. Permission is
     refused to allow mains high-voltage cables to run from the
     building to the motor, owing to the possible danger to the
     public. If the motor is situated close to a mains supply, show
     how you would solve the problem.

5   Draw a diagram of an electromagnetic relay with one-pole, two-
     way (single-pole, change-over) contacts. Label the important
     parts and describe how the relay operates.

The Uniselector

The uniselector is a multi-position relay which is sometimes
referred to as a 'stepping' relay. The common two-position relay
is a versatile device for children, but the uniselector broadens
the field of applications much further and is, therefore, worth
including in the course. No assignments dependent on this device
have been prepared, owing to its close relationship to the relay.
It is desirable, however, that children should see one or two
different types to compare physical size and number of positions.
Experience has shown that, if uniselectors are available, children
will make use of them in solving problems arising during project
work.

This shows a circuit diagram of a two-bank, ten-way (two-pole, ten-way) uniselector. If a supply is connected across the coil AB, the armature is actuated in a similar manner to that in a relay. This action causes a pawl to move to the next tooth on a ratchet wheel. When the supply is removed, a spring, which has been extended whilst the coil was energised, has the effect of pulling the switch over to the next position, since the switch wipers are attached to the same shaft as the ratchet wheel.

The spring steel latch prevents ratchet rotation when the coil energises but allows rotation under the action of the spring as the coil de-energises. A length of phosphor-bronze wire, or similar, rubbing on the wiper shaft serves as the pole of the switch.

The switch is continuous in action in that, in this case, when wiper X leaves contact position 10, wiper Y connects with contact position 1. If the uniselector has two banks, a second pair of wipers X^1 and Y^1 are fitted to the same shaft as wipers X and Y but wiper X   ratchet   wiper Y   switch pole connection

are insulated from them. Uniselectors having either eight banks and twenty-five ways or four banks and fifty ways are quite common.

Since the switch rotates continuously in only one direction, some means of quickly returning the uniselector wipers to contact position 1 is obviously desirable. This is achieved by making use of the 'homing' contacts. These contacts are operated by the armature.

When the coil is de-energised, the 'homing' contacts are closed; but when the coil is energised, mechanical linkage from the armature opens them. Thus, if the coil is supplied through these contacts, the armature will oscillate, as the contacts make and break, and the switch will rotate at a rapid rate.

rapid rotation

'homing' contacts

In order to stop the switch at position 1, one bank of the uni-selector is used as a 'homing' bank. All contacts except contact position 1 are connected together and wired as shown.

rapid rotation
to position 1

for external
switching

Using the same technique, the switch can be stopped at any position,
or even at a number of positions. A typical use of 'homing' is
shown below.

With the uniselector in position 1 (home) as shown, all lamps L_1 to
L_4 are extinguished. When switch S is impulsed, the uniselector
moves to position 2, illuminating L_1. At the next impulse, L_1 is

extinguished and L_2 illuminates; and so on to L_5. At the sixth impulse the device 'homes' to position 1.

A UNISELECTOR UNIT

A uniselector enclosed in a Perspex box with the pole contacts and coil connections wired to 4mm sockets is a useful addition to the basic equipment. A small uniselector of three banks, ten/twelve ways is particularly suitable. If the uniselector has more positions than this, internal 'homing' beyond position 10 could be arranged.

A typical layout:

poles—
yellow 4 mm
sockets

coil
direct

contact positions—
blue 4mm
sockets

coil via
homing
contacts

Perspex box

A homing bank can be conveniently arranged externally by linking switch positions by short leads fitted with stackable 4mm plugs.

ELECTRICAL-SWITCHING ASSIGNMENT 5

Capacitors can be used effectively for 'delaying' the operation of relays, and this assignment sets out to introduce pupils to this particular function of a capacitor. In the assignments, the capacitor is dealt with not from the standpoint of theory and construction, but in terms of its usefulness in control mechanisms.

Pupils observe what happens when a relay is connected across a supply and then disconnected. This shows quite clearly that the relay responds relatively quickly to the 'making' and 'breaking' of the supply. A capacitor is now fitted across the relay coil. When the supply is connected, the relay again energises in a very short time.

Relay energises quickly   Relay energises quickly

There is no discernible difference in the time taken for the relay to energise. When the supply is disconnected, however, the relay with the capacitor wired in parallel remains energised for a con-siderable time.

Relay de-energises quickly

Relay remains energised whilst the capacitor discharges. The discharge current is shown as a flow of negative electrons

Pupils will quickly realise that the capacitor stores electricity (electrical charge) when the switch is closed and gives up the charge to the relay coil over a short period of time after the

switch is opened. At the instant the switch is opened the
capacitor is already charged and has 12 volts across its terminals.
As it discharges the voltage falls. Eventually the voltage across
the capacitor plates is too low to drive sufficient current through
the relay coil to keep it energised. An alternative explanation is
that, at the beginning of the discharge, the discharge current is
high, and this falls off with time. At a certain low current the
relay de-energises. Theory and experiment show that the discharge
current falls off exponentially with time.

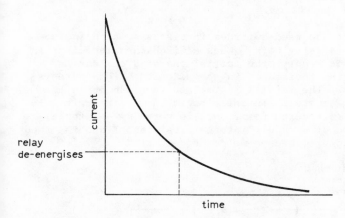

We do not mention this exponential decay yet. However, students
from now onwards will be using capacitors regularly, and at some
time the teacher should demonstrate the simple experiments mentioned
in appendix 3 -'Capacitors'.

Having established that a capacitor can 'delay' the de-energising
of a relay, pupils investigate the effect of using different values
of capacitor on delay time. Using the model vehicle, pupils
measure the distance that their vehicle reverses using, say, $2000\mu F$,
$5000\mu F$, and $10\ 000\mu F$ capacitors. The reversing distances should be
approximately proportional to the capacitance. The values are not
critical provided that they are whole-number multiples of the lowest
value. Capacitors of less than $500\mu F$ are likely to give only very
short reversing distances.

The reversing distances obtained when capacitors are connected in
series and in parallel will indicate to the pupils that the
effective value of two capacitors connected in parallel is the sum
of the two values. If two capacitors of equal value are connected
in series, the effective value is one half of the value of one of
them. Pupils may try connecting different value capacitors in
series, but we should not expect them to deduce

$$\frac{1}{C} = \frac{1}{C_1} + \frac{1}{C_2} + \ \text{---------} \ \frac{1}{C_n}$$

Points to Note

1   Pupils are warned in Assignment 5 to ensure that the capacitors
    are connected the correct way round, i.e. the positive terminal
    of the capacitor to the supply positive and the negative
    terminal to the supply negative.

2   The values of capacitors should be clearly marked. It is not
    necessary to define the 'farad', but pupils will discover from
    their experiments that, the greater the number of microfarads
    (μF), the larger the charge.

3   Pupils should not use reed-switches in circuits which include a
    capacitor across a relay coil. When a discharged capacitor is
    connected across a supply, the initial charging current is
    limited only by the resistance in the circuit. If this resis-
    tance is very low, the initial (surge) current can be in the
    order of several amperes. In the circuit shown, the critical
    current is high (since the resistance is very low - external-
    wiring resistance plus supply internal resistance) and the reed
    contacts are likely to become welded together.

The same argument is applicable to capacitor discharge, large
currents flowing if the external resistance is low.

90

Because of the large charging currents, a microswitch with
heavier contacts is used in preference to a reed-switch in
Electrical-switching Assignment 5.

4   The energising current for a relay is much higher than its
     'holding' current.

a strong magnetic field is   weaker magnetic field required
required to pull the armature   to hold armature down owing
over distance 'd' against   to proximity of armature
spring contacts   to coil core

This holding current varies not only between different types of
relay, but also between apparently identical types: the holding
currents of the RS type-40 relays suggested may vary by several
milliamperes. The consequence of this inconsistency is that,
for the same value of capacitor, pupils will find other vehicles
reversing for different distances. (Variations may also be due
to frictional factors in the model vehicles.)

5   The delay time of a relay is a function of its coil resistance
     in addition to the capacitor value employed; thus longer delay
     times can be achieved using relays with high resistance coils.

6   Electrical-switching Assignment 5 introduces a 'delay' caused
     by a relay remaining <u>energised</u> after the supply is removed.
     Relays can be made to remain <u>de-energised</u> for a short period
     after the supply is connected. The method is much more critical,
     but it may be of use in project work. A series resistor is
     employed.

            (a)   (b)

When there is no additional resistance R, see diagram (a), the capacitor charges rapidly when the switch S is closed, owing to the low circuit resistance. The uncharged capacitor has very low resistance initially, and 'short-circuits' the relay coil, but for only a very short time. In diagram (b) the capacitor now takes longer to charge, because of the additional resistance R. When the voltage across the capacitor plates has risen, the requisite energising current passes through the relay coil, and the relay energises.

By making the resistance R variable, the delay can be increased and decreased. If R is made too large, however, its resistance limites the circuit current to less than the relay energising current, and the circuit ceases to function.

CALCULATION OF SERIES RESISTANCE R

The RS type-40 relay has a minimum energising current of approximately 20 mA and a coil resistance of 185 Ω

Total circuit resistance = R + 185 Ω

If the supply voltage is 12V and the current required is 20 mA,

$$R = \frac{V}{I}$$

$$\therefore R + 185 = \frac{12}{20/1000}$$

$$\therefore R = \frac{12\ 000}{20} - 185\ \Omega$$

$$\therefore R = 600 - 185\ \Omega$$

$$= 415\ \Omega$$

Thus the maximum value for R is 400 Ω (approx)

If this value is exceeded the relay cannot energise. A 500 Ω variable resistor could be used to adjust the delay time.

Apparatus Required (15 pupils, 5 groups of 3)

five reed switch units

five microswitch units

five relay units (two-pole change-over)

five 2000μF capacitor units

five 5000μF capacitor units

five 10 000μF capacitor units

several miscellaneous capacitor units

five vehicles fitted with motor - made in Assignment 1

five power supplies - 12 V d.c., 5A - with safety fuse or trip

five 1 metre rules or similar

stackable 4mm plug leads - assorted sizes

Demonstrations

1   At an appropriate time, the charge and discharge characteristics
    of capacitors should be studied in more detail - see appendix
    3 - 'Capacitors'.

2   Discuss the effect of connecting capacitors in series and para-
    llel in the light of Electrical-switching Assignment 5.

3   Discuss factors affecting the energising current and minimum
    holding current for electromagnetic relays.

Buffer Experiment

Measure the vehicle reversing distance when capacitors of different
values are used. Plot a graph of capacitor value against distance.

Homework Questions

1   Draw a circuit diagram to show how you could arrange a lamp to
    be illuminated when a spring-loaded push switch is operated and
    to remain illuminated for several seconds after the switch is
    released.

2   In each case in the circuits shown below, the switch S is
    operated for a sufficient time to allow the capacitor to fully
    charge.

Which capacitor is storing the greatest charge and which the least?
What is the ratio of the charges stored by C_1, C_2, and C_3?

3 Indicate how the current flows in the circuit shown below at the instant the switch S is closed. Indicate the current flow in the circuit after the switch has been closed for some considerable time.

Give reasons for any answers you give.

4 In the circuits below, RL1 and RL2 are identical relays. Which relay remains energised for the longer time after switch S is opened? Give a reason for your answer. (If you are not sure of the answer, set up the equipment and test it.)

(a)   (b)

5 What is the effective capacitance in each of the following
   arrangements?

(a)

2000µF 2000µF

(b)

1000µF
3000µF

(c)

2000µF
5000µF
3000µF

(d)
3µF 3µF 3µF

ELECTRICAL-SWITCHING ASSIGNMENT 6

Later in the course, pupils will work on assignments involving
logic, logic circuits, and some important items of ancilliary
switching equipment known as <u>astable</u>, <u>monostable</u>, and <u>bistable</u>
devices.

Whilst these devices are often used in association with other logic
circuitry, they are useful items for use separately in the control
of equipment and operations. They are commonly referred to in this
way:

    astable - 'clock'

    monostable - 'delay'

    bistable - 'flip-flop'

Electrical-switching Assignments 5 and 6, with suitable demonstrations, deal with these three functions. Each device can be identified by its number of stable 'states', i.e. none, one, or two. For
example, a manual switch can be up or down, a relay energised or
not energised, a transistor may be conducting or not conducting. We
can simply call the states 'on' or 'off'.

In some switching systems, however, neither state (on or off) is
stable, and the system automatically switches itself from one state
to the other continuously. Such a system is referred to as astable
(without stability). The to-and-fro excursions of an astable
device beat out time at a definite frequency; the device is therefore analogous to the ticking of a clock. Pupils have already met
a kind of astable system in the form of the oscillating vehicle. By
completing Assignment 6, pupils are introduced to a relay oscillator
(refer to the notes on 'a double-relay oscillator' later in this
section).

A monostable system has one stable
state, as the name suggests. Again,
pupils have met such a system when
a capacitor is fitted in parallel
with a relay coil.

If an 'impulse' is applied by operating a spring-loaded switch S,
the relay energises and the capacitor simultaneously charges. When
S is opened, the relay remains energised for a time dependent upon
the charge stored in the capacitor. The stable state in this case
is when the relay is not energised, remaining so until an external
impulse is applied. The energised relay is then in an unstable
state, since it automatically de-energises when the capacitor has
discharged sufficiently. The term 'delay' is applicable to this
system, since there is a delay between the releasing of switch S
and the de-energising of the relay.

A bistable device has two stable states. Perhaps the simplest bi-
stable mechanism is a manual on-off switch such as a room lighting
switch; the switch remains indefinitely in one or other state   The
term 'flip-flop' is sometimes used because, when an impulse is
applied, the device 'flips' into one stable state but 'flops' into
a second stable state at the next impulse.

Electrical-switching Assignment 6 introduces pupils to a useful
bistable relay device.

A double-relay circuit is employed for three main reasons:

a) the inputs are in effect short circuits applied across X or Y -
    the possibility of damage to the unit is therefore less than if
    a supply voltage were used;

b) both inputs are identical, thus any method used to give input
    X can also be used to give input Y;

c) the circuit is closely analogous to transistor bistable circuits.

METHOD OF OPERATION

bistable unit - circuit diagram 1

Note: the numbers used are for the purpose of this description only
      and do not refer to any numbers printed on the relay type 44,
      nor to the numbered sockets, as given in the pupils' notes.

1   When the supply is first connected, both relays are de-energised
    (see circuit diagram 1). A short-circuit applied at X will
    cause relay A to energise, while a short-circuit applied at Y
    causes relay B to energise. Assuming sockets X are short-
    circuited, relay A energises and remains energised (even with
    the short-circuit removed) since its own contacts 7 and 9 are
    now joined, connecting the left-hand side of the relay coil A
    to supply negative through relay B closed contacts 13 and 14.
    The right-hand side of relay coil A and the left-hand side of
    relay coil B are permanently wired together and connected to
    supply positive (see circuit diagram 2).

    Any further impulses applied at X have no effect. Note that
    the external switch sockets (V) have now changed connections.
    External switch sockets (W) remain as before

97

bistable unit –
circuit diagram 2

2   If a short-circuit is applied at Y, relay B energises. Connection between contacts 13 and 14 is broken, causing relay A to de-energise, having lost its connection to supply negative. When relay B energises, 16 is connected to 18; and, when relay A de-energises, 4 is connected to 5, thus connecting relay coil B to supply negative. If the short-circuit at Y is now removed, relay B will remain energised (see circuit diagram 3).

circuit
diagram 3

Contacts V
1 and 2 joined

Contacts W
10 and 12 joined

A further short-circuit applied to Y has no effect. However, a short circuit applied at X causes both relays to change over again to the situation shown in circuit diagram 2, and so on.

98

Notes:

1   Either relay when on (energised) or off (not energised) is in a stable state.

2   The supply polarity can be reversed without affecting operation, i.e. the supply sockets need not be indicated positive and negative.

3   Except when the supply is first connected (or when there is no supply connected), one relay, and one only, should be energised (see note 4).

4   Inputs must be momentary short-circuits. If, for example, X remains short-circuited and a short-circuit is applied at Y, then both relays energise. This situation should be avoided, since the bistable action is lost.

5   An illuminated photocell, microswitch, etc. will operate as short circuits for the unit. In the case of a photocell, the 'impulse' must be caused by light striking the cell, not the action of breaking the beam to the cell.

6   The terms 'set' and 'reset' are commonly used when referring to bistables. When a short-circuit is applied at X, the bistable can be said to be 'set'; and when a short-circuit is applied at Y, it can be said to be 'reset'; and vice versa. These terms have little meaning unless the device is connected into an external circuit. The terms would have value, no doubt, in this case:

If microswitch A is operated momentarily, both relays change over and the lamp L is illuminated. Switch A has 'set' the circuit. To 'reset' the arrangement (i.e. to extinguish the lamp), the reset microswitch B is impulsed.

Pupils investigate the operation of the bistable unit in much the same way as they investigated the manual switch unit and relay unit, and summarise their findings in tabular form. Once familiar with the switching action, the pupils should be able to use the external switch sockets to make a vehicle reverse. The majority will no doubt at first fail to take into account that the situation is not quite the same as for relay switching. In a two-pole, two-way relay, <u>both</u> switches operate together (ganged); this gives the reversing circuit shown.

In the case of the bistable unit, either relay A or relay B is
energised, which results in the external switching sockets being
used as shown.

Most pupils should eventually appreciate the different arrangement
required after one or two unsuccessful attempts. If necessary, a
hint or two could be provided, but the solution should not be given.
Pupils should be asked to state what must be done to achieve
reversal of a d.c. motor, and they should be able to solve the
problem once they are clear as to what is required.

ALTERNATIVE ASSYMETRICAL BISTABLE (latched relay)

A bistable using only one relay is possible, but the impulse inputs
'set' and 'reset' are not identical.

When the battery switch is operated, S_1 is closed momentarily, and the relay energises. One set of its contacts immediately places a short-circuit across S_1, allowing the latter to be opened while leaving the relay energised. This could be the 'set' condition. To reset, the normally-closed switch S_2 is opened momentarily. This de-energises the relay and removes the short-circuit across S_1. When S_2 again closes, the relay remains de-energised until S_1 is again operated.

A TWO-RELAY OSCILLATOR

Although not included in the assignments, teachers should, if at all possible, allow pupils to attempt to make a relay oscillator. The problem could be stated as, 'Design and construct a circuit in which two relays form an oscillator by making and breaking the supply to each other.' Capable pupils will probably succeed in solving the problem. Each relay can operate a lamp to indicate time intervals when energised (or de-energised).

Pupils who do not attempt the design of an oscillator should at least see that the arrangement is possible (see 'Demonstrations').

Circuit for a two-relay oscillator:

Relays A and B are two-pole, two-way relay units. The values of capacitors C_1 and C_2 determine the switching frequency (frequency of oscillation), and values from $100\mu F$ to several thousand micro-farads can be tried. The effect of using unequal capacitor values for C_1 and C_2 should also be noted. Note that a pair of normally-closed contacts are used for one relay and a pair of normally-open for the other.

Method of Operation

When the on-off switch is closed, relay B energises immediately (and C_2 charges), since the right-hand side of relay coil B receives supply negative through contacts 4 and 5. Contacts 10 and 12 of relay B now close, thus energising relay A immediately (C_1 charges). With relay A energised, contacts 4 and 6 close, cutting supply negative to relay B. Relay B remains energised, however, until C_2 has discharged. Relay B then de-energises, disconnecting the supply to relay A as contacts 10 and 11 close. Relay A de-energises only when C_1 has discharged. When relay A de-energises, relay B energises immediately through contacts 4 and 5, and so on. Note that the supply polarity should not be reversed, otherwise the capacitors are wrongly connected.

SINGLE-RELAY OSCILLATORS

Single-relay oscillators are possible. A teacher may wish to investigate one or two and discuss them with pupils.

1 The speed of oscillation is limited by the mechanical construction of the moving parts (inertia).

2 Large 'mark-space' ratio, i.e. the relay is on for a time determined by capacitor C but off for a very short time.

3 Capacitor C keeps the relay energised for a period of time as in 2. The resistor R, however, delays the charging of capacitor C, thus delaying the energising of the relay. Equal mark-space ratios are possible, but, if the value of R is too high, it will prevent sufficient current flowing in the coil to

energise the relay. (Values
for approximately one-second
oscillation;   R.500 Ω variable;
C,5000 μ F; relay type 40 in
two-pole, two-way relay unit.)

WHAT DO WE EXPECT FROM PUPIL INVOLVEMENT IN ASSIGNMENT 6?

This will largely depend on the ability of pupils, but the following
is offered as a guide:

a) They should be aware of the bistable principle and understand
    the internal switching of the bistable unit as shown in the
    Assignment 6 Follow-up. They should not necessarily be expected
    to work out the circuit for themselves at this stage. They
    should be discouraged from attempting to memorise this or any
    other circuit; one aim of the course is to encourage pupils to
    design circuits by applying principles.

b) The pupils should make sufficient notes and diagrams to enable
    them to refer back to the principles involved should they require
    a bistable circuit as a control device in the future.

c) The terms 'set' and 'reset' should be introduced here and the
    associated concepts consolidated in later work.

d) Pupils should be aware of the single-relay bistable as a simple
    and cheap device which 'makes and breaks its own supply'.

e) They should be encouraged to draw a simplified diagram to repre-
    sent a bistable unit when the latter is used as part of more
    complex circuitry. At first, pupils may wish to use a simple
    diagram representing the unit, for example:

However, they should be encouraged to use a more general circuit such as:

They should not be expected to draw the complete bistable circuit at all times, although a teacher may ask for this on infrequent occasions to prevent the unit becoming a 'black box'.

f) Pupils should be able to recognise and construct a double-relay oscillator circuit and be able to explain how it works.

Apparatus Required (15 pupils, 5 groups of 3)

five relay bistable units

ten microswitch units (reed-switch units may also be used)

five vehicles fitted with motor, as made in Electrical-switching Assignment 1

five power supplies - 12V d.c., 5A - with safety fuse or trip

stackable 4mm plug leads - assorted lengths

ten suitable heavy obstructions, e.g. large blocks of wood, heavy weights, etc.

Demonstrations

1   Discuss the terms 'astable', 'monostable', and 'bistable', with the help of suitable equipment.

2   Discuss 'set' and 'reset' by assembling a suitable circuit, including two push-button switches (microswitch units held in the hand are suitable).

3 Demonstrate a single-relay bistable using a two-pole, two-way relay unit. (This could be investigated by pupils in order to produce, say, a burglar alarm.)

4 Discuss ways of drawing a bistable unit which is included in other circuitry.

5 Discuss the effect of applying a short-circuit to both pairs of green sockets. Show that the bistable action is then lost.

6 If pupils have not already attempted the task of producing a relay oscillator, the teacher should demonstrate and provide a circuit. Each group should then wire-up a similar unit.

Buffer Experiments

1 Attempt to design and wire-up a bistable unit using a single relay. Use a two-pole, two-way relay unit and two microswitches. The relay should energise when one microswitch is pressed, and should remain energised when the microswitch is released. The second microswitch should de-energise the relay when pressed, and the relay should remain de-energised when the microswitch is released.

Use a lamp indicator unit to assist you in determining whether or not the relay is energised.

Homework Questions

1 By reference to a circuit diagram (you will have one in your notebook, or use the circuit in Electrical-switching follow-up 6), describe how the two-relay bistable works.

2 What are meant by the terms 'astable','monostable', and 'bistable' in electrical and electronic circuitry.

3 What happens in the circuits (a) and (b) if the switches S are closed? Give reasons for your answers.

(a)   (b)

4   Draw a circuit diagram of a relay bistable device, using only
     one relay, and explain how it works.

ELECTRICAL-SWITCHING ASSIGNMENT 7

The photocell used in these assignments is of the light-dependent-
resistor type, the Mullard ORP12 being ideal. Although in later
assignments the photocell is used almost exclusively in a switching
capacity, this assignment establishes that, as the light falling on
the cell drops in intensity, the resistance increases, and vice
versa. This change in light intensity is achieved by varying the
distance between the light source and the photocell and noting the
effect on a lamp indicator unit placed in series with the cell. If
desired, a second indicator unit could be fitted directly across
the supply for comparison purposes.

(a)

Pupils connect a two-pole, two-way relay unit in place of lamp 2
and discover that the relay energises when light is incident on the
cell. The low resistance of the cell under illuminated condition
allows sufficient current to flow in the circuit to energise the
relay.

(b)

With the light-source unit placed 10 cm from the photocell unit
(measured by a metre rule placed alongside the equipment), lamp 2
(diagram (a)) in series with the cell glows brightly. As the

distance between the light source and photocell is increased, the brightness of the series lamp falls, showing that the circuit resistance increases. When the beam of light is shut off from the cell, by placing a hand in the light beam, lamp 2 is extinguished, showing an even larger rise in circuit resistance. With the end of the light-source tube in contact with the end of the photocell-unit tube, the resistance of the cell is in the region 20-50 Ω. In complete darkness (say when a hand is placed directly across the end of the photocell unit) the resistance rises to a value in excess of 500 000 Ω (500 kΩ).

Some pupils may wish to include an on-off switch at this stage; others may also wish to include a lamp indicator unit to establish the condition of the relay, and should be encouraged to do so.

For relay operation, the maximum reliable distance between the photocell and the light source is approximately 0.5m   Longer distances are often possible, but this depends to a large extent on the characteristics of the cell and relay. In later assignments a transistor/photocell arrangement allows a spacing of 3-4m. Stopping a vehicle when the light beam is broken should present little difficulty for students.

Notes:

1   The circuits recommended in the assignment sheets are designed to obviate any serious damage to the photocell. However, if a fully illuminated cell is fitted directly across a supply, or a piece of equipment with only a low resistance is placed in series with the cell, the cell will overheat and be irrevocably damaged.

2   The ORP12 has a maximum power dissipation of 250 mW. Assuming at a maximum illumination (light-source unit and photocell unit in contact end to end) the resistance of the cell is 10Ω (though it is likely to be a little higher than this), the power dissipated in the cell when placed directly across a 12V d.c. supply can be calculated as follows:

$$\text{power dissipated in cell} = \frac{V^2}{R} \text{ watts (or } I^2R \text{ or VI watts)}$$

$$= \frac{12 \times 12}{10} \text{ watts}$$

$$= 14.4 \text{ watts}$$

$$= 14400 \text{ mW}$$

The heat dissipated will burn out the cell.
The minimum series resistance permissible for 250 mW dissipation in the cell can be calculated similarly.

At a cell resistance of 10 Ω , the maximum current for 250 mW dissipation can be calculated:

$$power = I^2R \text{ watts}$$

$$\therefore \quad \frac{250}{1000} = I^2 \times 10$$

$$\therefore \quad I^2 = \frac{250}{10\ 000}$$

$$\therefore \quad I = 0.16 \text{ amperes (approx)}$$

$$= 160 \text{ mA}$$

Thus at maximum illumination (10 Ω resistance) the maximum current through the cell is 160 mA. In order to limit the current to this value, the total circuit resistance can be calculated as follows.

Assuming the supply voltage is 12 V d.c.,

$$R = \frac{V}{I}$$

$$\therefore \quad R = \frac{12}{160/1000} \Omega \quad (160 \text{ mA} = 160/1000A)$$

$$= \frac{12\ 000}{160} \Omega$$

$$= 75 \ \Omega$$

The circuit resistance when using a photocell must never fall below this value. Since the cell resistance can be as low as 10 Ω at maximum illumination, a further 65 Ω (75-10), at least, must be provided by a device placed in series with the cell.

In the Electrical-switching assignments, the following devices are used in series with a photocell:

a)   2-PCO relay unit - relay type 40 . . . coil resistance 185Ω

b)   bistable unit - relay type 44 . . . coil resistance 185Ω

c)   lamp indicator unit - 12 V, 2.2 W bulb . . . hot-filament resistance 65 Ω approx.

These figures show that no trouble should be experienced with relay units. With a series lamp unit, however, pupils should be discouraged from placing the light source and photocell units end to end, since the cell is then dissipating the rated 250 mW (approx). Some nominally rated 12 V d.c. power supplies will deliver more than 12 V, and thus the power dissipated in

the cell may exceed the maximum permissible.* For the above
reasons, pupils are asked to place the light source 10 cm from
the photocell and to note the effect when this distance is
<u>increased</u>.

3   A relay/photocell oscillator can be simply constructed by
making the contacts of a relay unit switch the light source on
and off.

When the supply is switched on, the light source illuminates
through the relay contacts 1 and 2.   The photocell resistance
falls and the relay energises.   On energising the relay, contact
1 connects to 3, extinguishing the light source.   The relay
therefore is de-energised.   Contacts 1 and 2 close again,
switching on the light source.   This sequence continues indefinitely.   The lamp indicator flashes on and off to show the
oscillation.   A capacitor fitted across the relay coil slows
down the oscillation.

Teachers may wish to demonstrate the arrangement and/or set it
as a buffer experiment.

Apparatus Required (15 pupils, 5 groups of 3)

five photocell units

five lamp indicator units (12 V, 2.2 W bulb) - if pupils use a
second unit for comparison purposes, then ten will be required.

five light-source units (12 V, 2.2 W bulb)

five power supplies - 12 V d.c., 5A - with safety fuse or trip

stackable 4mm plug leads - assorted lengths

five 1-metre rules

five two-pole change-over relay units

five vehicles fitted with motor - made in Electrical-switching
Assignment 1

---

*   The variation of filament resistance with temperature further
complicates the issue.   At low brightness the filament
resistance is less than 65 Ω .

Demonstration

Some teachers may wish to show the relay/photocell oscillator to the whole group at this stage.

Buffer Experiment

The relay/photocell oscillator assignment could be undertaken by a capable group: 'Connect a relay, photocell, and light source in such a way that when light strikes the photocell the relay energises, and at the same time the light source is switched off. To assist you in deciding what is happening, arrange for the relay to switch a lamp indicator on and off.'

Homework Questions

1   Fill in the blanks:

   a)   When light strikes a light-dependent resistor (photocell), the cell resistance .... When no light strikes the cell the resistance ....

   b)   A photocell is unsuitable for use in a .... atmosphere.

   c)   The inside of a photocell tube should be matt black to ....

2   Draw a circuit diagram to show how you would cut the supply to an electric motor when a beam of light is broken.

3   (For text see overleaf)

3 The circuit shown is intended to be used in an installation for
checking lengths of metal bar placed between A and B. If the
metal is short it must be rejected. Bars 2 m long or more are
acceptable.

The operator presses the push-to-make switch to make a test.

a) Describe in detail how the circuit works.
b) What is the purpose of L_1?

4 Draw circuit diagrams showing a light-dependent resistor (photocell) used as:

a) a switch, and
b) a variable resistance.

5 A photocell and light source can be used in conjunction with an
electromagnetic counter to find the speed of a motor shaft.
Describe how you would do this. Include a circuit diagram, and
explain how it works. (If you do not understand how an electromagnetic counter is constructed, you might ask to see inside
one.)

ELECTRICAL-SWITCHING ASSIGNMENT 8

This assignment should be attempted by more able pupils, but,
alternatively, it could be demonstrated to other groups.

Content

Pupils are asked to make their vehicle oscillate in and out of a
light beam, using a relay unit. This assignment should present
little difficulty, since the reversing circuit has been used
several times in previous assignments. However, when a capacitor
is fitted across the relay coil - 2500μF or so in the first
instance - a number of possibilities arise. The circuit chosen by
pupils will probably be:

As the vehicle approaches the beam, the relay is energised since light from the source is incident on the photocell. When the beam is broken, the relay remains energised because of the capacitor. The vehicle, therefore, continues moving in the same direction. What follows depends largely on the design of the vehicle, the speed of the vehicle, its shape, and the value of the capacitor. This is fully explained in the follow-up.

To summarise, the possibilities are:

1   If the vehicle moves fairly quickly, it will carry on through the beam until light again strikes the cell, and there will therefore be no apparent effect - the capacitor has not had time to discharge sufficiently.

2   Even if the vehicle is slow, the light may be broken inter-mittently, and the capacitor charges each time light hits the cell. Again there is no apparent effect, the vehicle continuing through the beam and beyond.

3   If the capacitor discharges through the relay coil by a sufficient amount while the light beam is broken, the relay de-energises and reverses the vehicle.

On leaving the beam, the relay (unexpectedly for the pupils) does
not energise immediately. If the photocell were a perfect switch
the relay would energise very quickly, but the finite resistance of
the illuminated cell, say 100Ω, delays the charge time and, therefore, the time at which the vehicle reverses. The vehicle may not
reverse again until it is several centimetres from the beam.

An explanation for delay times

The following is intended primarily for the information of the
teacher, though able pupils may benefit from a similar explanation.

Assuming that the capacitor has become discharged, when the switch closes, the capacitor now charges quickly (passes a large current). This short-circuit effect prevents an appreciable current flow in the relay, which therefore cannot energise immediately.

As a capacitor charges, its rate of charging diminishes.

This represents a gradual increase in the effective d.c. resistance of the capacitor; the coil of the relay is therefore shunted by an increasing resistance. Since resistors in parallel share the total current in inverse proportion to their respective resistances, the current in the relay coil rises as that in the capacitor falls.

When the effective resistance of the capacitor reaches a certain high value, the current in the relay coil is sufficient to energise the relay. When fully charged, the capacitor ceases to absorb charge and in effect becomes an open-circuit (infinite resistance).

The capacitor stores a definite amount of charge from the 12 V supply, and the time it takes to do so is determined by the resistance in the charge path. If this resistance is small, the initial charging current can be large and the effective capacitor resistance rises rapidly. Since the resistance of a mechanical switch and its wiring is very low, the capacitor charges almost instantaneously and the relay 'appears' to close immediately.

When the switch is opened, the capacitor discharges through the relay coil.

Photocell Capacitor charging:

Assume the cell is not illuminated and the capacitor has discharged through the relay coil.

When light strikes the cell, its resistance falls but still remains appreciable; the capacitor initial charging current is therefore limited. Since the capacitor is uncharged, it represents a short-circuit across the relay coil.

appreciable
resistance

negligible
current

fairly
large
current

12 V

The resistance of the capacitor depends upon its state of charge
and, since the charging current is limited, it remains a low resistance for an appreciable time, and there is a delay before the
relay energises.

Photocell Capacitor discharging:

When light is removed from the photocell, the capacitor discharges
through the relay coil.

Note: The rate of discharge also depends upon circuit resistance.
If the terminals are short-circuited, the capacitor discharges
almost instantaneously. However, the resistance in the discharge
path is the d.c. resistance of the relay coil, i.e. 185 Ω. Thus the
initial discharge current is limited, and a considerable time
elapses until the current falls to a value too low to maintain the
relay in an energised condition.

Apparatus Required (15 pupils, 5 groups of 3)

five photocell units

five light-source units

five two-pole changeover relay units

five vehicles fitted with motors - as constructed in Electrical-
switching Assignment 1

stackable 4mm plug leads - assorted lengths

five 2000μF, 25 volt capacitors

several assorted 25 volt capacitors, to enable groups to obtain
approximately 8000μF and 12 000μF by parallel connection.

five power supplies 12 V d.c 5A fitted with fuse or trip

Demonstration

1   For the less-able pupils the whole of assignment 8 should be
    demonstrated, or omitted completely.

117

2   For the above-average pupil, discuss the reason for vehicle
    behaviour as explained here.

Buffer Experiment

Set up the accompanying
circuit and observe the
effect of changing the
value of R (0 - 600 ohms
approximately).

Homework Questions

1   Draw a circuit diagram which would enable your vehicle to oscil-
    late in and out of a light beam. Describe the action of the
    arrangement.

2   The diagrams (a), (b), and (c) below show three similar circuits.
    the capacitors C in each are identical. The resistance of the
    resistor in (c) is twice that of the resistor in (b).

| (a) | (b) | (c) |

If the switches S are depressed simultaneously for a short time
and then released, which of the capacitors is likely to be
<u>storing</u>:

a)   the most charge, and
b)   the least charge?

3   The diagrams (a), (b), and (c) show three similar capacitor-
    discharge circuits. The capacitors C are identical in value
    and are holding the same quantity of charge. The resistance,

2X, of the resistor in (c) is twice the value of the resistor in (b).

| (a) | (b) | (c) |

If the switches A are depressed simultaneously for a short time and then released, which of the capacitors is likely to have <u>lost</u>:
a)   the most charge, and
b)   the least charge?

4   Complete the following:

When the supply is disconnected from a relay coil, the relay .... unless a ....is wired in parallel with the coil. The inclusion of this parallel ....keeps the relay .... for a time which depends upon the value of the .... the amount of ....it holds and the ....of the relay coil.

5   Describe and explain what happens when the light beam to the photocell in the circuit shown below is broken:

a)   for a short time,
b)   for a long time.

If a capacitor of about 2000µF were fitted across the relay coil, how would the circuit now behave?

This assignment should perhaps be demonstrated by the teacher to all
but the most able groups of children. At the end of Electrical-
switching Follow-up 8, the suggestion was made of using a second
relay to 'invert' the signal from a photocell. An illuminated
photocell causes a series relay to be energised; in Assignment 8
this is a limitation if an immediate vehicle reversal, followed by
a delay, is required. A capacitor fitted across a relay delays de-
energising appreciably, but not energising. In order to make the
vehicle reverse out of the light immediately, and reverse over a
short distance, the breaking of a light beam must <u>de-energise</u> one
relay which in turn causes a second relay to <u>energise</u>. This <u>second</u>
relay is delayed using a capacitor.

Immediately the vehicle breaks the light beam, RL1 de-energises.
RL2 then immediately energises and reverses the vehicle motor via
its reversing circuit. Once out of the light beam, RL1 again
energises, removing the supply from RL2 (switching is now as shown
in the diagram). RL2 remains energised for a while, however, owing
to the capacitor discharging through the coil. When discharged,
RL2 de-energises and the vehicle reverses towards the beam.

a) RL1 energised;
    RL2 de-energised.

b) RL1 de-energised;
    RL2 energised.

c) RL1 energised;
    RL2 energised via capacitor.

d) RL1 energised;
    RL2 de-energised
    (capacitor discharged).

Apparatus Required (15 pupils, 5 groups of 3)

*ten two-pole change-over relay units

five photocell units

five light-source units

five 4000μF, 25 V capacitors - any near value is satisfactory

five vehicles fitted with motor - as made in Electrical-switching Assignment 1

five power supplies - 12 V d.c., 5A - fitted with fuse or trip

stackable 4mm plug leads - assorted lengths

* If ten units are not available, some sharing will be necessary

Demonstration

This assignment should be demonstrated to all but the most able pupils.

Buffer Experiments

1   Using a similar circuit, make the vehicle reverse indefinitely when a beam of light is broken.

2   If four-pole change-over relay units are available, construct a symmetrical-input relay bistable unit using two four-pole change-over relays. (Can you remember the circuit? Probably not - but, before referring to your notes, try to set up the original circuit or any suitable alternative.)

Homework Questions

1   Describe the action of the following circuit on closing switch
    A: a)   when an obstruction is present, and
        b)   when there is no obstruction between the light source and the photocell.

2   For the circuit below, describe what happens to lamp L when the switch B is operated, returned to the un-operated position, and operated again.   Explain the behaviour of the lamp.

3   By means of suitable diagrams, show how a relay can be used:

a)   as an inverter,
b)   as a buffer.

4   A bell is required to ring approximately 10 seconds after a switch is pressed and to remain ringing for about 20 seconds, after which it must automatically stop.   Draw a diagram of a circuit to perform this function, and explain how it works.

5   Describe what you would expect to happen in the circuit below if light strikes one or both of the photocells A and B.   Give a reason for each of your answers.

ELECTRICAL-SWITCHING ASSIGNMENT 10

This assignment re-introduces the bistable unit, pupils again using
it to control their vehicle, but in this instance photocells are
used as switches in place of microswitches. This assignment should
be demonstrated to all but the more able children. Some pupils
might attempt the assignment in the normal way, but teachers should
first ascertain, however, that sufficient apparatus is available,
since the final circuit can be quite complex.

1   In the first part of the assignment the pupils connect a photo-
     cell across each pair of green sockets on the bistable relay
     unit (signal input sockets) and note the effect when the light
     beams to the photocells are incident on the cells, and when the
     beams are broken. The purpose of these tests is to emphasise
     again that an illuminated photocell (which is usually the
     'normal' photocell condition) behaves as a <u>closed</u> switch. The
     bistable unit does <u>not</u> behave as a bistable, however, since a
     requirement of the unit is that each green pair of sockets
     should receive a short-circuit only momentarily. Change-over
     cannot be achieved at the second pair of green sockets until the
     short-circuit has been removed from the first pair.

     Using photocells, the bistable unit behaves as follows:

     a)   Under 'normal' operation of a bistable relay unit <u>both</u>
           relays are never energised.

both relays energised

to 12 V supply

photocells

light sources

b) By moving the obstruction in and out of the beam to relay
A's circuit, relay A respectively de-energises and energises. Relay B is unaffected. Again this is 'abnormal'.

c) The effect is similar to that in (b) but in reverse. The
unit behaves 'abnormally'.

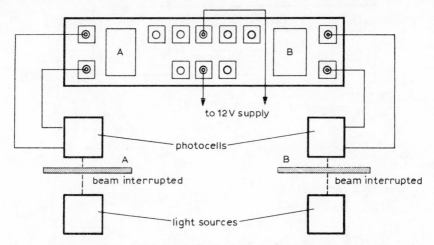

to 12 V supply

photocells

A   B

beam interrupted   beam interrupted

light sources

d)   In situation (d) the unit behaves 'normally'. If the
supply is switched on with both obstructions in place,
neither relay energises. If obstruction A is removed,
relay A energises and remains energised whether the
obstruction A is present or not. If obstruction B is
removed (with obstruction A back in position) relay B
energises and relay A de-energises. Relay B remains
energised whether the obstruction B is present or not.
By using the arrangement in this manner, the 'normal'
condition for each photocell is the un-illuminated
state (open-circuit switch). Short-duration short-
circuits are applied across each pair of green sockets
by removing the obstructions momentarily. This situation is analogous to the use of normally-open microswitches.

2   Once the reasoning above has been understood by pupils, they
should quickly realise that if photocells are to be used in
conjunction with a bistable unit, and if the photocells will
normally be illuminated, a relay must be incorporated in each
photocell circuit to <u>invert</u> the photocell signal. When each
beam is now <u>broken</u> in turn, the bistable will operate correctly.
See diagram (a) overleaf

Both relays are normally energised (photocells illuminated -
beams unbroken). Breaking a beam momentarily causes the associated relay to de-energise, momentarily placing a short-circuit
across one bistable input (the other input at this time being
open-circuited).

3   A vehicle can now be made to 'oscillate' between two beams of
light, since the motor reverses direction each time a beam of
light is broken. See diagram (b) overleaf

(a)

(b)

<u>Notes</u>:

1   In the above circuits, more than one 12V supply has been shown. In practice only one would be used, but pupils should be encouraged to show separate ones in any complex circuit diagram, as greater clarity can be achieved by doing so.

2   When pupils test the bistable unit in the first part of this assignment they should be encouraged to connect a pair of lamp indicator units to the bistable-unit external-switching sockets, to indicate the states of the relays.

Apparatus Required (15 pupils, 5 groups of 3)

five bistable relay units

*ten two-pole change-over relay units

 ten photocell units

 ten light-source units

 five vehicles fitted with motor - as made in Electrical-switching Assignment 1

 five power supplies - 12 V d.c., 5A fitted with safety fuse or trip

 stackable 4mm plug leads - assorted lengths

 ten lamp indicator units

 * If ten units are not available, some sharing will be necessary.

Demonstration

As has already been suggested, for all but the more able children, the whole of this assignment should be demonstrated. If the teacher wishes it, all could read through the assignment, and one group of children set up the equipment, taking into account suggestions from the rest of the pupils.

Buffer Experiments

1   The following circuit enables a bistable relay to operate from a single input. Set up the arrangement and test it. A single input bistable should change-over at the first input pulse and change back again at the next pulse. In this case the pulses are short-circuits provided by switch S.

How do you think the performance of the circuit is affected by:

a)   the length of the input pulse,
b)   the time between pulses?

Homework Questions

1   A photocell can be used in a switching capacity. Does such a
    cell behave as a 'closed' or as an 'open' switch:

    a)   when the cell is illuminated, and
    b)   when the cell is not illuminated?

    Why is a photocell not quite as good a 'switch' as a mechanical
    type?

2   Describe and explain how you would set up a circuit consisting
    of bistable relays, a relay oscillator, an electromagnetic
    counter, and any other apparatus you need, in order to time how
    long it takes to walk or run 100 m.

3   A traffic-light system, consisting of red and green lights only,
    is often used when road works prevent the use of both sides of
    the road. Devise a suitable circuit to control a set of lights
    for this purpose, and describe how it functions.

4   A burglar alarm is required for your school. Design a suitable
    system and explain how it works.

Linear motion

GENERAL INTRODUCTION

It is recommended that the pupils tackle this section after completing the mini-projects which follow the Electrical-switching Assignments.

During the course so far, pupils have been concerned primarily with rotary motion, but in future project work linear motions may be required for a number of purposes - e.g. feeding, spacing, rejecting, steering, clamping mechanisms, etc. - and these assignments are designed to make pupils <u>aware</u> of the various methods available and to enable them to <u>select</u> the most suitable system for a given design requirement.

Pupils are asked (in Assignment 1) to think of as many ways as possible of converting rotary motion to linear motion and then to select one of their ideas, construct a Meccano version, and test it. Fortunately, the range of Meccano components enables most of the commonly used mechanisms to be assembled with little difficulty. A wide range of solutions should be encouraged, to enable the properties of the various systems to be compared.

However, it is unlikely that all the linear-motion problems to be met in later project work can be solved satisfactorily by using an electric motor and a standard mechanism of some kind; for instance, if a large force is to be applied then a very robust mechanism is essential, which might well cause constructional problems and operate unsatisfactorily. However, such a force can be provided conveniently and efficiently by means of a pneumatic (or hydraulic) cylinder; whilst if a short fast movement is required this might be better produced by means of a solenoid. It is therefore considered desirable that pupils should have the opportunity of using components such as solenoids and pneumatic cylinders to enable efficient and realistic solutions to be produced.

Pressure Units

Pneumatic pressure gauges were traditionally calibrated in lbf/in^2 or kgf/cm^2 but are now calibrated in 'bars', as this is the unit adopted by industry.

However, the SI unit of pressure is N/m^2, which would give extremely large values for the pressures used - normal operating pressure would be approximately 550 000 N/m^2.

The 'bar', which is approximately equal to 10^5 N/m^2, would provide a convenient unit giving a gauge scale range of 0-6 bars, but would introduce difficulties with the calculations in Assignment 3.7 when considering pressure, force, and diameter relationships.

After careful consideration it has been decided to use, in this course, the unit of N/mm^2, which simplifies the calculations considerably and gives a reasonably convenient gauge scale range of 0-0.6 N/mm^2.

Also, since $1N/mm^2$ is approximately equal to 10 bars or 10kgf/cm^2, a gauge calibrated in either bars or kgf/cm^2 is easily converted to N/mm^2.

Approximate pressure equivalents:

At the time of writing, few cylinders are made with metric diameter bores, but eventually all cylinders will be metrically dimensioned. Until metric cylinders are readily available, approximate metric equivalents of imperial dimensional cylinders will prove satisfactory for the linear-motion investigations,

e.g. ½" = 12 mm dia.
     ¾" = 18 mm dia.
     1" = 24 mm dia.

These approximations maintain the proportional increases yet keep the calculations simple.

Assignments 2 and 3, in which the pupils investigate the properties of solenoids and pneumatic cylinders, have two main aims. Firstly, the pupils discover the operating characteristics of both the solenoid and the pneumatic cylinder. This knowledge, together with that gained from the mechanisms discussed in Assignment 1, should enable them to select a suitable system for a particular application.

Secondly, Assignments 3.1 - 3.7 provide suitable training and experience in the investigational approach. Since this is the first time that pupils have been required to carry out quite difficult investigations, considerable guidance is essential if results are to be satisfactory. Although the assignment should ensure that each investigation is tackled in methodical steps, it is advisable for each pupil to study the notes entitled 'The Approach to Investigational Experiments', before attempting any of Assignment 3.1 - 3.7.

In most of the investigations, pupils are asked to draw a graph from the results obtained. Most pupils are able to draw reasonably good graphs, but very few are able to interpret them and draw suitable conclusions. For this reason, pupils should refer to 'The Use of Graphs', before the investigations are attempted. It is not intended that pupils should 'learn' the contents at this stage, but they should read through the notes in order to be aware of the essential points.

As a result of carrying out these investigations, the pupils should:

a) become more methodical in their work,

b) improve their powers of observation,

c) learn to use and read instruments more accurately,

d) learn to take more than one reading to ensure suitable accuracy,

e) record results in a clear tabulated fashion,

f) draw graphs from their results if necessary,

g) produce suitable conclusions from analysing the results - this is particularly important.

Thorough training in these techniques should help the pupils in future investigational work, in analysing ideas for project work, and in everyday-life situations.

For Assignment 2, commercial types of solenoids should be available for the pupils to examine.

For Assignments 3.1-3.3 the special multi-tapped solenoid is recommended. The power supplies and switch units used in the Electrical-switching assignments are suitable for use with the solenoids.

The provision and use of pneumatic cylinders and associated equipment might present some initial problems. However, it is considered important that pneumatic equipment is made available because:

1 Comparatively large forces are easily obtained, e.g. a 25mm diameter cylinder produces at a working pressure of say $0.6N/mm^2$ a force of approximately 250N - a typical feed force for drilling a 4mm diameter hole in a piece of mild steel.

2 Pupils are made aware of the industrial application of the equipment, and can solve relevant problems in a realistic way.

3 Pupils are provided with a wider range of techniques with which to solve problems.

4 In principle, pneumatic components are very similar to hydraulic components, and references can be made to the use and advantages

of hydraulic systems. However, in using pneumatic components one avoids the danger of the high forces produced by hydraulic systems and the possibility of burst pipes and leaks. With the pneumatic system, used air escapes to the atmosphere, whereas all used hydraulic fluid must be returned to the pump.

5   With the addition of fluidic sensors, which provide very sensitive detecting facilities (analogous to photocells etc.), pneumatic systems can be used in a wide range of situations.

6   Logical circuitry can be applied to both pneumatic and fluidic systems.

Since pneumatic valves are analogous to electrical switches, pupils having completed the Electrical-switching assignments, experience little difficulty in using the new equipment.

Although pneumatic equipment is rather expensive, the components are quickly taken apart and used again and again. They are very robust in construction and should give many years of reliable service.

Safety

In addition to the obvious dangers of trapping parts of the body between mechanisms operated by compressed air, attention should be drawn to two further hazards.

1   Very series bodily damage can arise if compressed air is misused, e.g. an open pipe directed into an ear etc.

2   Long pipes, when disconnected at one end, swing about dangerously when carrying high-pressure air.

These two dangers can be minimised by introducing the following circuit into the main supply.

To activate the circuit, push-button A is pressed, which, via the shuttle valve, provides primary air supply to the push side of the cylinder and, as discovered in Linear-motion Assignment 3.6, equal pressure on each side of the piston of a double acting cylinder causes the piston rod to move out slowly.

When the piston rod activates valve B, air is supplied to the external circuitry and also to the cylinder via the shuttle valve. Valve A may then be released because, if there is sufficient back pressure from the external circuitry, the piston rod will continue to activate valve B. However, if the outlet pipe is disconnected there will be insufficient pressure applied to the push side of the piston and the piston rod will retract, releasing valve B and therefore cutting off the air supply. Also if pipes are disconnected from the external circuitry with the pressure on, the supply will be cut off. To restore the supply, pipes must be re-connected, valve A held down until the piston rod again activates valve B, then valve A released.

Admittedly, air pressure is supplied to the external circuitry whether pipes are connected or not if valve A is held down, but on releasing this valve the supply is cut off and this should provide adequate protection.

By using a 25 mm dia. cylinder a difference of approximately 0.03 N/mm^2 between supply pressure and output pressure is detected, which provides protection against disconnected pipes but does not cause the supply to be cut off under normal working conditions. Because the circuit detects differences between supply and output pressures, it will operate at all but the very lowest supply pressures.

The most satisfactory means of obtaining compressed air is by means of an electrically driven compressor incorporating a storage tank. (The hydrovane compressor does not require a tank; it is therefore much lighter, but unfortunately much more expensive.) A capacity of at least $0.1m^3$ is required and an operating pressure in excess of $0.3N/mm^2$ (normal working pressure is usually $0.6N/mm^2$). It is strongly recommended that a compressor with automatic pressure control is obtained.

To cut costs, a second-hand compressor might be considered, or the assembly of separate components, e.g. a compressor driven by a cheap second-hand electric motor with the addition of a pressure switch, storage tank, etc. This will be a satisfactory solution only if the equipment is reliable, otherwise a great deal of frustration will occur.

Some schools with good workshop facilities may be tempted to make some pneumatic components (cylinders etc.) to reduce costs, but this is not recommended as it is unlikely that such equipment would prove satisfactory. Absolute reliability of all components used in the course is considered essential if the pupils are to gain the confidence necessary to achieve success in the more complex project work.

The hiring of bottles of compressed air (NEVER OXYGEN because of the oil present in the valves and cylinders) is another possibility. If a suitable regulator and gauge are available, this may be a satisfactory solution in the short term.

It is considered essential throughout this course that pupils handle the equipment, investigate possible applications, and also use it to solve the problems confronting them in later project work.

Unless a source of compressed air and a range of valves and cylinders are available for practical work, it is strongly recommended that the section involving pneumatic equipment is omitted: it is debatable whether one should talk about equipment unless it is available for the pupils to handle, investigate, and use.

A compressor, together with a range of pneumatic components, might be shared by a number of schools, each school using the equipment for a half-term or so. Initially, this may seem to be a satis-factory solution, as it would allow pupils in each school to cover the basic work in pneumatics, but the pupils would be deprived of the equipment when tackling their own project problems. Unless the pneumatic equipment is available during the whole period of the project (constant experimentation and testing is usually required once the initial ideas have been formulated), one should question, perhaps, whether to undertake the assignments involving the use of pneumatic components.

Choice of Pneumatic Components

There are many manufacturers of pneumatic components, several of whom make components suitable for use in this course. Factors to be considered include:

1   COST

Expensive, well-made components are generally more reliable than cheaper versions; but, as all are guaranteed to operate for a million or more cycles of operation, the cheaper valves are satisfactory for school use.

2   SIZE

If the pneumatic components are to be used in conjunction with Meccano, or in the construction of working devices of limited size, the components themselves must be small. 12mm (½") cylinders have been used successfully, and even smaller ones are available. Valves are sometimes difficult to accommodate, but a microswitch operating a solenoid valve could be used, or alternatively the sensing can be carried out by fluidic devices.

134

3   SHAPE

It is essential that the components can be easily fixed into position, and those having several fixing holes are more satisfactory.

4   SCREWTHREADS

Unfortunately, components supplied by different manufacturers may not be compatible, because a variety of screwthreads are used. It would appear that the BSP screwthread may eventually become standard, but at present at least three threads are used. Adaptors can be obtained to make all connections compatible; these add to the initial expense, but do prevent improperly connected fittings from damaging the ports and rendering an item useless. A damaged adaptor can be replaced cheaply.

5   PIPES

Nylon pipes are essential, and several types of fitting are available. All methods are quite satisfactory, but it must be remembered that, during this course, pipes will be connected and disconnected far more frequently than during industrial applications. A pipe fitting which protects the end of the pipe will probably prove most satisfacotry.

Some manufacturers of suitable pneumatic components are:

Enots Ltd   Maxam Power Ltd
PO Box 228   Camborne
Birmingham B6 4ST   Cornwall

Kay Pneumatics   A Schrader's Son
London Road   Fluid Power Products
Dunstable   Walkmill Lane
Beds   Bridgetown
                              Cannock
                              Staffs

LINEAR-MOTION ASSIGNMENT 1

In this assignment, pupils are asked to devise means of transforming rotary motion to linear motion. All pupils should be able to suggest at least three methods, and some may produce as many as six or seven. Some pupils may encounter difficulty in putting ideas on paper because their diagrams become unnecessarily complicated.

It may be advisable to give some hints on how to represent various components to enable simple line diagrams to be made, for example:

guide

pivoting joint

sliding component
showing movement

spring

It is important that as many different ideas as possible are developed; this will provide training for later project work, when alternative methods of solving a problem must be explored. To achieve this, it is essential that a certain time (20-30 minutes) is given to section 1, during which time no pupil is allowed to proceed with section 2. Without such a restriction, some pupils, eager to build a model, will be satisfied with one or two obvious solutions and will not give the problem sufficient thought.

When the teacher is satisfied that section 1 has been satisfactorily completed, he may wish to ensure that a number of different solutions to the problem are constructed. If two groups wish to construct the same system, one of them could be encouraged to be more ambitious and to attempt a different solution. Experience has shown that it is possible for five alternative solutions to be produced with little or no direction from the teacher.

The results obtained from sections 3, 4, and 5, depend upon the ability range of the pupils; the teacher may consider that sections 1 and 2 provide sufficient involvement and challenge for his pupils.

When the construction work and tests have been completed, it is suggested that each group demonstrates its own version, giving details of constructional problems, advantages and disadvantages, etc. This approach not only provides a great deal of information, but it gives the pupils an opportunity to talk about their work. The boy with limited verbal ability may have useful information about a mechanism he has made.

Whilst some of the facts in the follow-up will have been dealt with, it is suggested that the teacher and the class should look through the notes together, so that further explanations can be offered.

A few notes from the follow-up may be desirable, but these should be kept to a minimum - the aim of this assignment is to make pupils aware of the various systems, to help guide their choice of mechanisms in the future.

Apparatus Required (15 pupils, 5 groups of 3)

five Meccano motors

assorted Meccano angle, strip, angle brackets, gears, wheels, nuts and bolts, etc.

additional Meccano items:

rack strips	(part no.110 or 110a)
slide pieces	(no. 50)
eccentrics	(no. 130 or 130a)
fork pieces	(no. 116 or 116a)
slotted strips	(no. 55 or 55a)
corner brackets	(no. 133)

five 1kg weights

With the above equipment, the following mechanisms can be constructed:

a) crank and slider,
b) peg and slot
c) eccentric,
d) rack and pinion.

Demonstrations

1   If a particular mechanism has not been constructed, and the teacher feels that the pupils should be able to see exactly how it operates, e.g. the peg-and-slot mechanism, a model should be made and demonstrated later.

2   It is very important that, having constructed Meccano models, pupils should also be shown how the mechanisms are used in engineering. It should be possible to find examples for demonstration purposes when the follow-up is being studied

Examples which should be readily available include:

a) Crank and slider
    Car or motor-cycle piston, gudgeon pin, connecting rod, and crank-shaft

b) Peg and slot
    Shaping machine

c) Cam and follower
    Car or motor-cycle valve gear

d) Eccentric
    Model-steam-engine valve gear; some types of paper punch

e) **Rack and pinion**
Hand-operated carriage movement on lathe; feed mechanism of bench drilling machine; car steering box

f) **Screwthread**
Vice; car-jack; lathe leadscrew

Buffer Experiments

1 In the screwthread and rack-and-pinion systems, the rotation must be reversed to change the direction of movement. Using such an arrangement, driven by an electric motor, devise a method of making the moving part reciprocate backwards and forwards continuously.

2 Provide a screw-type car-jack. What is its velocity ratio?

Homework Questions

1 Velocity ratio = $\dfrac{\text{distance moved by effort}}{\text{distance moved by load}}$

Mechanical advantage = $\dfrac{\text{load}}{\text{effort}}$

Efficiency = $\dfrac{\text{MA}}{\text{VR}}$ x 100%

250 mm

200 N

In this example the screwthread has a 'lead' of 1mm, i.e. in one revolution the nut moves 1mm along the bolt.

If the efficiency of the 'system' is 15%, calculate the force produced.

2 In a four-stroke petrol engine, each valve opens once for every four strokes of the piston. Make a simple sketch of the main components of the engine, showing clearly the valve-operating mechanism.

3 Compare the cam and eccentric mechanisms. What are the advantages and disadvantages of each?

138

4   When the steering wheel of a car is turned, the rotary motion
    is converted to linear motion by the steering box. Make a sketch
    of the mechanism you would prefer to use for a steering box.

5   From the graph shown below:

    a)   What is the minimum distance that the ram projects from
         the machine?

    b)   What is the maximum projection of the ram? How many
         seconds are required to reach this position?

    c)   What can you say about the speed of the ram between A and
         B and between B and C?

    d)   Between what times is the ram moving at its greatest speed?
         Calculate this maximum speed.

    e)   At what time is the ram projecting 50mm from the machine
         on its return journey?

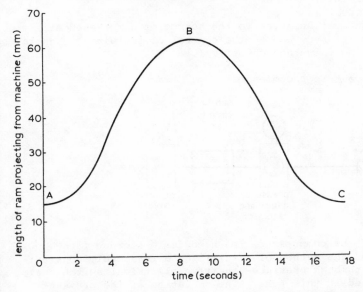

6   Account for the differences in the shape of the two graphs
    shown below.

Graph of crank-and
-slider mechanism

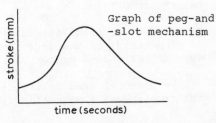

Graph of peg-and
-slot mechanism

This assignment introduces the pupils to solenoids and pneumatic cylinders, the properties of which will be thoroughly investigated in Linear motion 3.1-3.7.

Pupils are asked to examine the construction of various solenoids and pneumatics cylinders provided, and to operate each through the appropriate power supply in order to establish basic properties. Some groups may wish to carry out some simple testing at this stage, and this should be encouraged, provided that the tests are simple ones.

For this assignment, and for Linear motion 3.1-3.7, it is unlikely that sufficient apparatus will be available to allow five groups to attempt the same investigation. It is suggested that three sets of pneumatic equipment and three sets of electrical equipment are provided, and that the class is divided into the usual five groups. (The spare set should ensure that pupils waste little time in waiting for apparatus.)

Some introduction must be given to the source of compressed air, whichever system is used, and to the control of the air through the pressure regulating valve and on-off valve.

The following layout is recommended:

The operation of the compressor, the need for a storage tank and safety valve, and the method of maintaining a reasonably constant-pressure supply through pressure-sensitive electrical switches etc should be outlined at this time. The operation of the pressure regulator should be demonstrated: there is a need, when reducing pressures, to reduce further than necessary and then to increase to the required value.

Stress that airtight joints can be made without excessive tightening of components; if too great a force is applied the fittings may be damaged, or indeed broken.

It may be considered desirable to provide further information on the construction of a pneumatic cylinder, e.g. the position, shape, and material of the airseals. Since the construction will vary, for specific details consult the manufacturers' catalogues. However, it is felt that the principles of construction are more important at this stage than individual design features.

Apparatus

commercial solenoids of different sizes and types

12V d.c. power-supply units

on-off switch boxes

leads

single-acting pneumatic cylinders of various diameters and strokes

double-acting pneumatic cylinders of various diameters and strokes

connecting pipes

a source of compressed air with regulator and gauge, with three on-off valves for take-off points.

Demonstrations

1   Demonstrate and explain the operation of the pneumatic equipment.

2   Demonstrate the use of the regulator - if reducing the pressure, reduce below the value required, and then build up the pressure.

3   Demonstrate the type of pipe fittings used, emphasising that over-tightening may cause damage or breakage. The method of making up a pipe could also be demonstrated if necessary.

4   Demonstrate various applications illustrating the use of solenoids and pneumatic cylinders, e.g. a relay, an electric bell, a vehicle trafficator, a pneumatic door control.

5   Films dealing with the use of pneumatic equipment in industry are available from the manufacturers of pneumatic equipment.

Buffer Experiments

1 Replace the solenoid armature with:

    a)   a piece of brass rod of the same diameter,
    b)   a piece of aluminium rod of the same diameter,
    c)   a piece of steel of approximately half the diameter of the original armature.

In each case record your observations and, if possible, give an explanation for the results.

2 Operate a pneumatic cylinder at various air-supply pressures. Estimate the effect the change in air pressure has on the force produced.

Homework Questions

1 Produce sketches showing some applications of solenoids and pneumatic cylinders with which you are familiar.

2 Compare the movements produced by:

    a)   the armature of a solenoid,
    b)   the piston rod of a single-acting pneumatic cylinder,
    c)   the piston rod of a double-acting pneumatic cylinder.

LINEAR-MOTION ASSIGNMENTS 3.1-3.7

Refer the pupils to the notes on 'The Approach to Investigational Experiment' and 'The Use of Graphs' before any of these assignments are attempted.

To be completed successfully, these investigations demand skill in setting up the apparatus, accurate observation and measurement, thorough and orderly recording of results, and the ability to reach a reasoned conclusion.

Pupils should be encouraged to:

a) check their results by taking more than one reading (averaging the readings if necessary);

b) tabulate the results, if appropriate;

c) record accurately what they observe, whether it appears 'correct' or not;

d) draw graphs to establish relationships;

e) develop meaningful conclusions.

Experience has shown that initially pupils find these investigations difficult, but they make good progress once familiar with the apparatus and the techniques involved.

It may be advisable to partially demonstrate investigations 3.1 (solenoid) and 3.4 (pneumatic cylinder) before the pupils attempt any assignment, to ensure that the basic essentials are fully appreciated from the start.

Pupils should be allowed to work through these investigations at their own rate; some will finish all seven (and the buffer experiments) during the time others take to complete three or four. Providing all pupils have successfully tackled a number of investigations, and have developed the necessary techniques, it is suggested that the teacher demonstrates the remaining investigations, to prevent holding up the faster workers. A general discussion of results should follow, and some general conclusions concerning the properties of solenoids and pneumatic cylinders should be developed and recorded.

The teacher should repeat Assignment 3.1, this time using a solenoid with a steel insert (bolt). Whilst this investigation may have been attempted by some of the faster workers (as a buffer experiment), it should now be demonstrated to all, and the effects discussed in detail. This is the form of solenoid that the pupils will invariably use in later projects.

The follow-up should provide all the information required, although results may vary slightly from those indicated. Since the apparatus used is relatively crude, it is wise not to interpret the results too rigidly.

It should be remembered that the main purpose of these assignments is that:

a) pupils appreciate certain properties of solenoids and pneumatic cylinders;

b) pupils develop the skills required to carry out investigational work which in future may not be so clearly directed.

Apparatus

SOLENOID INVESTIGATIONS 3.1-3.3

Apparatus required per group:

    one multi-tapped solenoid unit
    one graduated armature
    one 0-100 gram (0-1N) spring-balance
    one retort stand with two clamps
    one switch box
    one 0-2A ammeter
    one variable resistor
    one 12V power supply
    five leads

Apparatus required per group:

    either   a) 12mm dia. double-acting cylinder with 0-100N spring-
                 balance and frame mounted on a board

    or   b) 18mm dia. double-acting cylinder with 0-100N spring-
                 balance and frame mounted on a board

    or   c) 24mm dia. double-acting cylinder with 0-250N spring-
                 balance and frame mounted on a board.

Note: The stroke of each cylinder must be adequate to extend the
spring-balance over the working range.

Details of frame and mounting board

Dimensions will depend upon cylinders and spring-balances available.

one air-pressure supply
one regulator and gauge
one on-off valve
one pipe

Ideally each group should have its own regulator and pressure gauge;
but it is possible for three groups to work together from one gauge,
though each will need an on-off valve (as suggested for Linear-
motion 2).

For investigation 3.6, each group will need a tee-junction and
three connecting pipes.

Demonstrations

1   Set up and partially demonstrate assignments 3.1 and 3.4 before
    these investigations are attempted by pupils.

2   Some of the later investigations could be demonstrated, to
     enable the slower workers to catch up.

3   Repeat investigation 3.1 using a solenoid fitted with a steel
     insert. Record and discuss the results.

Buffer Experiments

1   Repeat investigation 3.1 using a solenoid fitted with a steel
     insert.

2   Using a cylinder of known piston diameter, measure the diameter
     of the piston rod and by experiment establish the frictional
     forces when (a) pushing, (b) pulling.

Homework Questions

1   A solenoid fails to produce an adequate pull force. Suggest
     how this can be increased (a) without altering the solenoid,
     (b) by re-designing the solenoid.

2   A double-acting pneumatic cylinder has a piston of 50mm
     diameter and a piston rod of 10mm diameter. Draw a graph of
     pressure against force for this cylinder to enable you to read
     off the theoretical (ignoring friction) push and pull forces
     for all pressures up to $0.6N/mm^2$.

3   A pneumatic cylinder has an effective piston diameter of 40mm.
     The air pressure applied is $0.7N/mm^2$. The average frictional
     force is 80N. What force is exerted by the piston rod? (Take
     π to be 22/7.)

4   The armature of a relay constructed in the school workshops
     fails to move away from the coil when the latter is
     de-energised. What could be the reason for this? Suggest how
     the relay could be made to function correctly?

5   The diagram overleaf shows part of a car braking system. What
     force is applied to each pad of the disc brake?

force 500 N

200 mm

50 mm

master
cylinder
40 mm dia

two cylinders
each 30 mm dia

disc

Pneumatic control

In the Linear-motion assignments, the pupils investigated the
properties of pneumatic cylinders. Further knowledge and experience in the use of pneumatic-control equipment is now required.

To help pupils appreciate the similarity between pneumatic and
electrical circuits, reference is made throughout these assignments,
to the equivalent electrical components and electrical circuits
used in the Electrical-switching assignments.

Symbols

The symbols used in these assignments are <u>not</u> the recommended
British Standard symbols (BS2917: 1969) but a form used earlier by
a number of manufacturers of pneumatic equipment. The earlier
symbols are considered to be more suitable in this course since
they are very similar to the standard electrical symbols with
which the pupils are already familiar. Their use emphasises the
similarity in function of the components, for example:

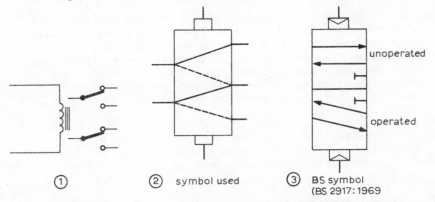

① electrical symbol

② symbol used

③ BS symbol
(BS 2917: 1969)

pneumatic symbols for identical component

unoperated

operated

There is no doubt that for the professional engineer the BS symbols
are preferable, because the condition of the valve and the direction
of the air flow are both clearly shown. Since pupils immediately
accept the similarity between the function of electrical and
pneumatic components, though, to use the BS symbols would involve
them in mastering a more difficult form of representation, which is
less effective at this stage.

In this course it is considered essential that design problems are
first solved in principle and then the appropriate constructional

medium is chosen. It is believed that this approach is more likely to succeed as a result of emphasising the similarity of the alternative systems.

Equipment

For guidance on the compressed air supply and other equipment, refer to the teachers' notes on Linear motion.

The use of a combined filter and regulator is recommended, but a lubricator is not considered essential (in fact, it must <u>not</u> be used with fluidic components) since components are unlikely to need lubrication when used for relatively few operations. Dust entering the valve ports is more likely to cause unreliable operation.

Types of valve

Two types of valve are particularly suitable for the work undertaken in the course:

a)   the poppet valve,
b)   the spool valve.

THE POPPET VALVE

The poppet valve mechanism consists of a ball held against a seal by means of a spring; operation is achieved by holding the ball away from the seal. In this type of valve the air supply must be connected to the inlet port so that the continuous air pressure assists the spring in holding the ball against the seal. Air can flow from the inlet to the cylinder connection only when the valve is operated, and from the cylinder to exhaust when unoperated.

The advantage of this valve over the spool type is that frictional resistance is minimal and therefore actuating forces are comparatively low, which makes it particularly suitable for use as a 'sensor', i.e. converting mechanical movement to air-pressure change.

These valves are referred to as 'on-off' valves.

THE SPOOL VALVE

In this type of valve, a spool (basically a cylindrical rod with a number of annular grooves cut in it) is moved to control the flow of air. Because of the friction between the spool and the sealing rings, these valves require actuating forces two to three times greater than those for the poppet-type valves.

The function of the ports of the spool valve may be interchanged, for example:

With the air supply connected to:

a) the inlet port -air pressure is directed to the cylinder when
    the valve is actuated (normal use);

b) the exhaust port - air pressure normally flows to the cylinder
    but is cut off when the valve is actuated (the inverse of (a));

c) the cylinder port - air pressure normally flows to the exhaust
    port, and to the inlet port when the valve is actuated.

The three-port valve shown is used in each of the above ways in
Assignment 4.

In these assignments, the three-port spool valve is referred to as
a 'single change-over valve', and the five-port as a 'double change-
over valve', to emphasise the fact that the pneumatic valves perform the same function as the electrical switches used in the
Electrical-switching assignments.

Actuators

Both the 'poppet' and 'spool' valves are available with a wide
range of actuators (see Assignment 1).

Approximate operating forces/pressures:

Actuator	Spool valves	Poppet valves
Push button/plunger	40N	12N
Roller operated	20N	6N
Lock-down lever	10N	3N
Double pilot	$0.15N/mm^2$	-
Single pilot, spring return	$0.3N/mm^2$	$0.1N/mm^2$
Diaphragm, spring return	$0.05N/mm^2$	$0.02N/mm^2$

Working Pressures

It is recommended that normal working pressure be in the region of
$0.4-0.6N/mm^2$ - it must be in excess of $0.3N/mm^2$, since this
pressure is required to operate a pilot air-actuated, spring-return
spool valve.

Note:

If using air stored in a reservoir to operate a valve, as in
Assignment 4, always use a diaphragm valve, for the following
reason:

When valve A is operated, air from the reservoir at $0.5N/mm^2$ flows
through the pipe to valve B. With the increase in volume there is
a corresponding fall in pressure. If the pipe is long there may be
insufficient pressure to operate valve B. In this case use a
diaphragm-actuated valve at B, which will operate at pressures as
low as $0.02N/mm^2$ (this point is made in Follow-up 4).

Conversely, in the circuits in Assignment 5, a high-pressure operated valve is required, e.g. a pilot-operated spring-return spool
valve, to enable a reasonable time delay to be obtained.

Organisation

With limited pneumatic equipment, it is likely that only one group
can be involved in practical work at any one time; there is then
a temptation for the teacher to merely demonstrate all the investigations. This should be avoided if the pupils are to become
familiar with the equipment, handle it with confidence, and succeed
in getting the circuits functioning correctly. The essence of
teaching through assignments is pupil involvement.

However, in Assignment 6, pupils first analyse a complex circuit
and after assembly check their conclusions. It would be very time-
consuming for five groups of pupils to assemble this complex circuit
so it is suggested that all groups first study the circuit and that
the assembly is carried out later as a class activity.

150

Since a certain amount of recording is involved, one set of equipment can be shared by two groups, one 'writing up' while the other is doing the practical work. The other groups can be involved with other assignments, as it is not necessary, at this stage of the course, for all pupils to work through the same assignments simultaneously. Therefore, while some pupils work through the Pneumatic-control assignments, others can be occupied on the Fluidic-control assignments, Resistance, or Rectification assignments. However, assignments should be tackled in the recommended order, e.g. the Resistance and Rectification assignments must be completed before the Transistor assignments are attempted.

Special Demonstrations

With groups working on different assignments it is impracticable to give special demonstrations to the whole class. Also, at this stage, pupils have greater experience of investigational work, and the assignments themselves include more detailed experiments which at the beginning of the course might have been teacher demonstrations It seems unnecessary to include any special demonstrations in this section.

However, a visit to a local factory to see the use of pneumatic equipment, or the showing of a film on industrial applications might be considered.

Buffer Experiments

Groups will now be working at their own pace and on completion of one assignment will move on to the next. However, some buffer experiments are suggested which might be useful on completion of this section of the course.

Homework Questions

A selection of questions appears at the end of this section.

Overall Aim of the Assignments

To provide sufficient knowledge and experience in the use of pneumatic equipment to enable pupils to solve practical problems which might arise in project work. Pupils should be able to devise and assemble appropriate pneumatic circuits.

PNEUMATIC-CONTROL ASSIGNMENT 1

Aims

1   To familiarise the pupils with the on-off poppet valve, the various types of actuators available, and the symbol for each

2   By a series of investigations to help pupils appreciate that
    the double-acting cylinder produces a useful force only if one
    side of the piston is exhausted while pressure is applied to
    the other. (To move the piston in the opposite direction the
    conditions must be reversed, and in this connection the term
    'change-over' is introduced.)

3   To introduce the principle of speed control.

Apparatus per group

one single-acting cylinder

one double-acting cylinder

two hand-operated on-off poppet valves

range of valves showing various types of actuators

one tee junction

five connecting pipes

PNEUMATIC-CONTROL ASSIGNMENT 2

Aims

To introduce methods of controlling a double-acting cylinder:

1   By using a hand-operated, five-port double change-over valve.

2   By impulses from two hand-operated valves, in conjunction with
    a double pilot-actuated double change-over valve.

3   To provide automatic oscillation by positioning valves which
    are actuated by the piston rod itself.

4   To provide full control of the cylinder by inserting two extra
    valves to enable the piston rod to be stopped in either the
    retracted or the extended position, and to operate for one
    cycle only.

Apparatus per group

one double-acting cylinder (plus two nuts to fit the piston rod)

one hand-operated five-port double change-over spool valve

one double pilot five-port double change-over spool valve

one single pilot spring-return valve (for inspection only)

two lock-down on-off poppet valves

one roller-actuated on-off poppet valve

152

one plunger-actuated on-off poppet valve

one cross junction

ten connecting pipes

PNEUMATIC-CONTROL ASSIGNMENT 3

Aims

To achieve control of piston speed of both double-acting and single-acting cylinders using exhaust restrictors and flow-control valves.

Apparatus per group

one double-acting cylinder) the larger the diameter, the
one single-acting cylinder) greater the degree of control

one double pilot five-port double change-over spool valve

one plunger-operated on-off poppet valve

one roller-operated on-off poppet valve

two exhaust restrictors

one flow-control valve

one cross junction

eight connecting pipes

PNEUMATIC-CONTROL ASSIGNMENT 4

Aims

1   To introduce the three-port single change-over valve as an inverter (similar function to the relay used in Electrical-switching Assignment 3).

2   To introduce the air reservoir and its use in pneumatic circuits.

Apparatus per group

one single-acting cylinder

one single pilot spring-return three-port spool valve

one reservoir

one lock-down on-off poppet valve

one diaphragm-actuated on-off poppet valve

one exhaust restrictor

one cross junction

one tee junction

eight connecting pipes

PNEUMATIC-CONTROL ASSIGNMENT 5

Aims

To investigate further circuits involving the use of a reservoir
and flow-control valves.

Apparatus per group

one single-acting cylinder

one flow-control valve

one reservoir

one single pilot spring-return three-port spool valve

one lock-down on-off poppet valve

two tee junctions

seven connecting pipes

PNEUMATIC-CONTROL ASSIGNMENT 6

In this assignment a complex circuit is presented for analysis.
This will test the understanding of the previous work.

If sufficient equipment is available it is recommended that the
pupils connect up this circuit in order to check their conclusions.

Follow-up 6 suggests an alternative circuit - a circuit more likely
to be used in industry. This employs sequence switching; the completion of one operation causes the next to commence - in this way
the correct sequence of operations is always maintained.

Apparatus Required

one single-acting cylinder

one double-acting cylinder

one push-button on-off poppet valve

one plunger-actuated on-off poppet valve

one single pilot, spring-return three-port spool valve

154

two double pilot three-port spool valves

one double pilot five-port spool valve

three reservoirs

two flow-control valves

two exhaust restrictors

two cross junctions

six tee junctions

twenty-four connecting pipes

For the circuit in Follow-up 6, the following additional equipment is required:

one plunger-actuated on-off poppet valve

one one-way trip-actuated on-off poppet valve

HOMEWORK QUESTIONS

1   Draw a diagram of a pneumatic circuit which will produce a delay between the time of operating a valve and the resulting movement of a single-acting pneumatic cylinder. How can the delay time be varied?
If the maximum duration of this delay is to be increased, what modifications would you make to your circuit?

2   When a push-button valve is given an impulse, the piston rod of a double-acting cylinder is required to move out slowly and remain fully extended for three seconds before retracting quickly. Design a circuit to achieve this.

3   What will happen when valve A in the circuit above is switched on? Explain fully the operation of the circuit.

4   In the circuit shown below, which valves must be operated to make the piston rod extend?

5   When an impulse is applied at valve A in the circuit below, the piston rod should immediately extend, and retract after a delay. What component is missing?

6   What will happen when valve A is switched on in the circuit shown below? Explain fully the operation of the circuit.

full flow

7   A door, operated by a double-acting pneumatic cylinder, is required to open when a person approaches it, and to remain in the fully open position for five seconds before closing. If other persons approach the door before it closes, it must remain

fully open for five seconds after the last person has passed
through.

Design a pneumatic circuit to achieve this.

BUFFER EXPERIMENTS

1 a)   Connect up two lock-down on-off valves to a cylinder as
        shown below.
        Explain why this circuit is unsatisfactory.

   b)   i) Investigate the properties of a shuttle valve by
            connecting one valve and cylinder as shown below.

         ii) Remove the valve and connect it to the other port of
             the shuttle valve.

        iii) Connect a valve to each of the shuttle-valve ports;
             you now have a similar circuit to that of (a). Is
             this satisfactory?

         iv) Can you suggest uses for this valve?

2   The circuits given in Homework questions 3, 5, and 8 could be
     made up to verify the pupils' explanations.

3   The pupils' circuit designed in Homework questions numbers 1, 2,
     and 7 could be connected up and tested.

Fluidic control

Low-pressure air-operated devices used in fluidic control have no
moving parts, yet provide switching facilities.

Several methods have been developed to provide the switching, the
two principles in general use being:

a)   the wall-attachment device,
b)   the turbulence amplifier.

The second system has been selected for use in this course because:

a)   the unit is simple,
b)   its operation is easily understood,
c)   operating pressures are low, and therefore air consumption is
     kept to a minimum.

In this course, the fluidic equipment is used initially in conjunction with the pneumatic equipment to provide a wider range of
sensing devices.   Later the equipment can be used in various
applications of logic for control purposes.

BASIC REQUIREMENTS

A wide range of equipment is currently available, and selection is
made difficult by the continuous introduction of new items.

By making use of the available pneumatic equipment, the following
arrangement reduces initial costs.

A means of setting the pressure via the precision controller is essential - a suitable pressure gauge, with overload protection, is available, but it should be possible to reduce costs further by means of a home-made manometer. A second gauge is desirable as it enables the input and output pressures of a sensing device to be compared, and it is also useful for finding faults.

COMPONENTS REQUIRED

one precision controller   Norgren 11-918-999
one(two) 0-500mmwg pressure gauges (0-20 wg)   Maxam 7089A06990
one bank turbulence amplifiers   Maxam 7089P99914
two ultra-sensitive valve operators   Norgren 5DA-921-10A
(to operate standard pneumatic valve)
6m nylon tubing, 2.4mm (3/32") bore   Maxam 7071A01240
3m nylon tubing, 1.5mm (1/16") bore   Maxam 7071A01230
ten Y connectors for 1.5mm bore tubing   Maxam 7089B00800
ten output tubes for interruptible jet   Maxam 7089B00400
ten input tubes for interruptible jet   Maxam 7089B00380
two car brake-light indicator switches (to
convert pneumatic pressure to electrical
output)

A manifold is also required to distribute the low-pressure air to the sensing devices. It is suggested that this is manufactured within the school, since it is relatively simple to make.

Manifold

holes to provide push fit for
2·4mm bore nylon tubing

drill to receive output
from precision controller

SENSING DEVICES

These are simply and cheaply made using the interruptible-jet tubes.
Some designs are shown below.

Interruptible jet

input

output

vee to locate
tubes in alignment

clamping
plates

Air-stream detector

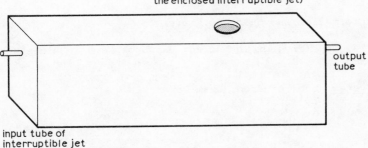

hole for the entry
of the air stream

(vertically above the gap in
the enclosed interruptible jet)

output
tube

input tube of
interruptible jet

161

Pressure-sensing head

this could be made
from a block of clear Perspex

holes to suit 2·4 mm
bore nylon tube

If finances permit, the following alternatives might be considered.

The Maxam step-up relay unit (7089P99882) may be used in place of the combination of the Norgren ultra-sensitive valve and the standard pneumatic valve.

A low-air-pressure-operated electric relay is available (Maxam 7089P99907).

Complete sensing devices are also available.

Interruptible jet   (Maxam 7089P99954)
Air-stream detector   (Maxam 7089P99921)

SUPPLIERS

Maxam Power Ltd
Camborne, Cornwall

(branch offices in London, Birmingham, Bristol, Sheffield, Manchester, Glasgow.)

Norgren Fluidics
C.A. Norgren
Shipston-on-Stow
Warwickshire

For further information and guidance, refer to:

Introducing Fluidics (Project Technology Handbook No.4), Heinemann Educational Ltd.

The Maxalog System, booklet from Maxam Power Ltd.

Electronics

The purpose of this section of the course is to extend the pupils' knowledge of basic electrical and electronic circuitry in order that they may later devise suitable circuits for control purposes.

The basic-electronics assignments are divided into three sections: Resistance assignments, Rectification assignments, and Transistor assignments. Use is made of a specially designed turntable in a number of these assignments. While some of these would need only slight modification in order to dispense with this turntable, replacing it with a motor fitted with a gearbox, the unit serves two important functions:

a) as the basis for mini or minor projects which a teacher may wish to set during the period - the turntable being a convenient unit involving, say, the removal of articles after being detected during sorting, counting, selecting, etc.;

b) to enable pupils to make preliminary investigations and to try out selected solutions to a major group project attempted at the end of the Transistor assignments - details of this project are given later.

Note: Buffer experiments are not included in these notes. At this stage in the course, the more capable pupils should be able to devise their own additional work.

RESISTANCE ASSIGNMENT 1

Initially, pupils would be asked to assemble the turntable units, but teachers may decide to leave them assembled after teaching the course for the first time. Pupils should always check that gears are meshing correctly and that there is correct freedom of movement at bearing surfaces.

This assignment is concerned primarily with a simple method of reducing the speed of a d.c. motor by using resistors of various values in series with the motor. Pupils discover that the effective resistance of two resistors placed in series is the sum of the individual resistors.

The potential-divider principle emerges from the results of the various investigations, and the follow-up indicates how a variable resistor can be used to give a variable output voltage from a fixed-voltage supply. The limitations are not discussed, though teachers should be aware of them. The two main disadvantages are explained below with the help of diagrams

A

B

i) Diagram A shows that, whenever a potential-divider is set up, a current I_1 is taken from the supply, irrespective of whether or not current is being delivered to an external circuit.

ii) Diagram B shows the effect when an external circuit is added. A second current path is produced, I_2 representing the current taken by the device L. If the slider is central, resulting in equal resistances above and below it, then with no load (diagram A) the voltage appearing across both X and Y will be 6V, since the currents in X and Y are identical.

p.d. across X = I_1 x R

p.d. across Y = I_1 x R

When an external circuit is completed, however, as when supplying an electric motor from the divider, an additional current flows in X but not in Y. Thus the p.d. across X must now be greater than that across Y, say 8V and 4V respectively, and the output voltage falls. The output voltage of a potential-divider network is, therefore, very sensitive to the current taken by the device being supplied.

Apparatus Required (15 pupils, 5 groups of 3)

five turntable units, either in kit form or completely assembled

five power supplies - 12V d.c. 5A - with safety fuse or trip

ten multimeters, or five 0-20V voltmeters and five 0-1A ammeters

ten 25 ohm resistor units

five 50 ohm resistor units

stackable 4mm plug leads - assorted lengths

164

Demonstrations

1   Show pupils a variety of wire-wound resistors - fixed and variable. Discuss the reasons for the differences in size.

2   If pupils are not familiar with the use of a multimeter, then demonstrate its use now, leaving ohmmeters until Assignment 2.

Homework Questions

1   Describe the assembly of a turntable unit, pointing out any precautions which must be taken during its assembly.

2   Explain why the speed of the motor on the turntable is reduced when a resistor is placed in series with it.

3   A resistor of 100 ohms is placed in series with a 12 volt motor. If, while running, the motor has an effective resistance of 200 ohms, what voltage appears across the motor?

4   Two 12 volt motors are fitted in series across a 12 volt d.c. supply,

    a)   How will the speed of each motor compare with the speed of such a motor placed directly across a 12 volt d.c. supply?

    b)   If a voltmeter is fitted across each of the motors placed in series, what is each meter likely to read?

    c)   What is the effect if the two motors in series are placed across a 24 volt d.c. supply?

RESISTANCE ASSIGNMENT 2

Pupils are asked to compare the resistance of a light-source filament when cold with its resistance when hot. They later use a variable resistor to control the speed of an electric motor.

The ohmmeter is introduced as a direct means of resistance measurement, and suitable meters should be available. Teachers should demonstrate to the class how these meters are used.

The follow-up draws attention to the limitations of variable-resistance motor control, namely that the high starting current required by the motor results in a low voltage supplied to it at this time.

Apparatus Required (15 pupils, 5 groups of 3)

five turntable units

five power supplies - 12V d.c., 5A - with safety fuse or trip

five 0-20V voltmeters

five 0-1A mmeters

five lamp ndicator units

five 100 ohm variable-resistor units (or similar)

five ohmmeters giving an appreciable reading for 100 ohm (one would
be sufficient if passed round to each group)

stackable 4mm plug leads - assorted lengths

Demonstrations

1   Demonstrate the use and discuss the construction of an ohmmeter
    to support the assignment notes.

2   Demonstrate the use of a variable resistor, connected as a
    potentiometer, on an a.c. supply. Show that the a.c. output
    voltage - as measured on an a.c. voltmeter - varies with the
    position of the slider in a similar way to d.c.

3   Demonstrate the use of a potentiometer as a volume control in
    a radio receiver. In this case the AC signals from the receiver
    appear across the whole control, the output being taken between
    one end and the slider.

Homework Questions

1   How does the resistance of the filament of a tungsten lamp vary
    with its temperature? Such lamps eventually 'blow' when they
    are first switched on. Why is this?

2   When an ammeter is placed in series with an electric motor and
    a power supply, the motor speed falls slightly.

    a)   Give an explanation for this.

    b)   Is the reading on the ammeter a reliable indication of
         the current taken by the motor when first connected to
         a 12 volt d.c. supply? Provide an explanation.

3   Imagine you have been given a milliammeter with a blank scale.
    Describe how you would make an ohmmeter from the instrument,
    and describe one way of roughly calibrating it, assuming you had
    a supply of accurate resistors.

4   You are given a 12 volt d.c. power supply, a variable resistor,
    and a 12 volt electric motor. Draw circuit diagrams to show
    how you would connect the variable resistor, firstly as a rheo-
    stat and secondly as a potentiometer. One of the arrangements

is less likely to enable you to stop the motor or to run it at full speed. Which one is this, and why?

RESISTANCE ASSIGNMENT 3

In this assignment, pupils compare the output voltage of a mains-operated low-voltage power supply with that of a lead-acid accumulator under different loading conditions. They should notice that the output voltage falls with increasing current demand; this is evident when using a mains unit even if relatively small currents are delivered to a load. This 'loss' of voltage from a power supply may suggest to pupils that there must be a resistance 'built into the supply' which forms a potential-divider with the external load. The follow-up explains the effect in detail.

This assignment also introduces the principle of 'power rating'. It is essential that pupils should be aware of heat generation in electronic apparatus whenever electrical energy is converted into heat energy.

Apparatus Required (15 pupils, 5 groups of 3)

five power supplies - 12V d.c. 5A - with safety fuse or trip

five 0-20V voltmeters

five high-current solenoids (one or two may be sufficient)

one fully charged lead-acid accumulator, 12V car-battery capacity

ten 25 ohm resistor units (5W) } 25 ohm, 50 ohm, 75 ohm, and 100
five 50 ohm resistor units (5W) } ohm can be obtained from these

five 10 ohm, approx. ¼W carbon resistors (expendable)

five 10 000 ohm, ¼W carbon resistors

stackable 4mm plug leads - assorted lengths

Demonstration

Discuss the precautions which must be taken when using photocells in series with a low-resistance device. For instance, one of the Electrical-switching assignments suggests fitting a photocell and lamp indicator unit in series with a 12 volt supply. Under this arrangement the cell is working at almost maximum heat dissipation. A higher current lamp could cause the cell to be damaged.

Homework Questions

1   The circuit over page shows a photocell fitted in series with a lamp and a 12 volt supply. When the cell is illuminated, the resistance of the cell is 60 ohm and that of the lamp 120 ohm.

a) How much current flows in the cell and in the lamp?

b) What voltage appears across the cell and across the lamp?

c) If the cell is rated at 0.25 watt (250 mW), is it likely to be damaged?

2   An electric fire is connected to a 250 volt mains and carries a current of 4 amperes. What is the wattage rating of the fire?

3   A 3 kW electric kettle is connected to a 250 volt supply. What current is drawn?

4   The electric motors you use sometimes become warm. Why is this, and under what kind of conditions is it likely to 'overheat'?

RESISTANCE ASSIGNMENT 4

The resistor colour code is introduced as a means of identifying values of resistors used in electronic equipment, the code being mainly used for the low-wattage types. It is not envisaged that pupils will memorise the code, but it should be made available for easy reference.

Pupils try connecting resistors in parallel, to determine the effective value of the arrangement. The relationship is not easily deduced, and a method of calculating the effective resistance of a parallel (shunt) arrangement is given in the follow-up.

Apparatus Required (15 pupils, 5 groups of 3)

fifty colour-coded carbon resistors of assorted values and toler-ances. If preferred, use five sets of ten assorted types in order that each group has the same values, though this is not essential. Use a large spread of values from less than 10 ohm to a few megohm; tolerance values should include 5% (gold band), 10% (silver band), 20% (no band), and if possible 1% (brown band) and 2% (red band).

five 50 ohm resistor units (5W)

five ohmmeters giving large readings in the region of 100 ohm

stackable 4mm plug leads - assorted lengths

Demonstrations

1   With more able groups, show that the colour coding of capacitors is similar to that for resistors.

2   Discuss the components in a chassis containing electronic components. Identify resistors, and discuss their values and likely wattage ratings.

Homework Questions

1   You have a supply of 10, 20, and 50 ohm resistors. Using these values only, describe the arrangements you would use to obtain resistances of:

   a)   30 ohm,
   b)   5 ohm,
   c)   125 ohm.

2   a)   The coil in a relay unit has a resistance of 185 ohm. What current does the relay coil carry when it is connected across a 12 volt supply?

   b)   Explain as fully as you can why any two relays may have different resistances.

3   A colour-coded resistor has red for the first digit, violet for the second, and orange for the multiplier.

   a)   What is the nominal value of the resistor?

   b)   If the tolerance band is coloured gold, between what two values of resistance would the actual value fall?

4   A 100 ohm, ¼W resistor is placed directly across a 12 volt supply. Is the resistor likely to overheat?

RECTIFICATION

Students will have been using low-voltage, mains-operated power-supply units during the course, but little has been said so far concerning the construction of such equipment. This section is intended to enable pupils not only to understand power-supply circuitry but also to enable them to construct a power-supply unit, should the need arise. While it is not recommended that pupils should construct mains power supplies, owing to the danger involved with high voltages, it is possible that, during project work, d.c. will be required from a low-voltage a.c. source.

INTRODUCTION - THE USE OF THE CATHODE-RAY OSCILLOSCOPE

Little needs to be said concerning this combined assignment and follow-up except to stress that oscilloscopes capable of accepting d.c. inputs are essential. In the assignments that follow, oscilloscopes capable of displaying only a.c. are suitable, but, in order to give students an understanding of the principle of the oscilloscope, direct-current voltages are investigated in this first instance. If only one d.c. instrument is available, then this could be demonstrated.

Apparatus Required (15 pupils, 5 groups of 3)

one cathode-ray tube from an oscilloscope, or an oscilloscope with the cover removed in order that the tube can be seen (the latter is less satisfactory, since the tube will be shrouded in a mu-metal screen.)

five oscilloscopes, with at least one having facilities for d.c. inputs; pupils must use the d.c. input type for investigation 5.

five batteries to give 'pure' d.c., preferably 6 to 12 volts, though 1.5 volt torch cells could be used.

stackable 4mm plug leads - assorted lengths. Ensure that pupils can make good electrical connections to the oscilloscope inputs if these are not 4mm size.

Demonstrations

1   If possible, show the pupils a cathode-ray tube of the type used in an oscilloscope (electrostatic-deflection type), pointing out the relevant parts. If this is not possible, remove the cover from an oscilloscope in order to see the tube.

2   If only one d.c. input oscilloscope is available, teachers may wish to demonstrate 5 and 6, though it is more satisfactory to allow the pupils to attempt these sections themselves.

Homework Questions

1   Assuming that a focused spot is required at the centre of an oscilloscope screen, which controls would you adjust if you observed the following:

a)   the spot is central on the screen but is blurred?

b)   the spot is sharp but positioned to the left of centre (at nine o'clock)?

c)   the spot is sharp but positioned above centre (at twelve o'clock)?

d)   the spot is sharp but dim and positioned at two o'clock?

2 An oscilloscope is set up so that there is a horizontal line on the face of the tube. If it takes 0.01 seconds for a spot to trace out this line,

a) how long does it take to trace out half of the line?

b) how many lines are traced out each second?

3 An oscilloscope is set up with a line on its screen. Draw a diagram to indicate the change of position of the trace if,

a) a 3 volt battery is fitted across the Y input terminals, with the oscilloscope adjusted for d.c. inputs;

b) the 3 volts is increased to 6 volts, then to 12 volts.

4 A spot is placed centrally on the screen of an oscilloscope. The circuit below is set up, and the output is connected to an oscilloscope as shown. What would you expect to see on the screen when switch S is closed?

RECTIFICATION ASSIGNMENT 1

Assignment 1 introduces the transformer and the diode, and the unidirectional property of the latter is investigated by the pupils. For the first time, pupils briefly connect a d.c. motor to an a.c. supply and note the effect. The resulting vibration, rather than continuous motion in one direction, should lead pupils to conclude that the motor is attempting to rotate first in one direction and then in the other. This conclusion is confirmed when the diode is placed in series with the a.c. supply. This 'device' first appears to block that portion of the alternating supply which produces current flow in one direction, and then, after reversal, that part of the alternating supply which causes current to flow in the other direction. Teachers should ascertain that all pupils have a clear understanding of alternating current at the completion of this assignment.

Apparatus Required (15 pupils, 5 groups of 3)

five transformer units (mains input, 12-0-12V output)

five turntable units - assembled

five power supplies - 12V d.c., 5A - with safety fuse or trip

five oscilloscopes

five 50 ohm resistor units (5W)

five diode units

five 0-20V voltmeters

stackable 4mm plug leads - assorted lengths

Demonstration

Exhibit different types of diode when pupils have completed the
assignment. Show low-current as well as high-current types. If
possible, show the older type of 'finned' metal diode (rectifier).
Discuss the relative sizes, e.g. semiconductor diodes of the type
used in the diode unit are considerably smaller than the 'finned'
selenium type. If possible, also compare the physical size of valve
rectifiers with semiconductor diodes of the same current-carrying
capacity.

Homework Questions

1 A 12V, 0.1A bulb is fitted into a lamp indicator unit and the
   latter is then placed across the 12 volt output of a transformer connected to the 240 volt mains. What current flows in
   the primary coil of the transformer?

2 The primary coil of a transformer has 2000 turns, and the secondary 50 turns. If the primary coil is connected to the 240 volt
   mains, what voltage is obtained from the secondary?

3 A diode is suspected of being faulty. Describe how you would
   use an ohmmeter to test it. What kinds of readings would you
   expect on the meter if:

   a)   the diode is 'good'?

   b)   the diode is faulty?

4 In the circuit shown below, what are the possible causes if:

   a)   the motor 'buzzes'
        but does not
        rotate?

   b)   the motor does not
        'buzz' or rotate?

172

RECTIFICATION ASSIGNMENT 2

One cannot expect pupils to 'discover' or design a full-wave rectification circuit, and in this assignment, therefore, circuits for
full-wave and full-wave 'bridge' rectification are given. Comparisons are first made between the waveforms obtained from half-wave,
full-wave, and full-wave 'bridge' circuits. Each supply in turn is
connected to the turntable motor, and it will be noted that the two
full-wave circuits result in very similar motor speeds; but the
motor runs noticeably slower when using the half-wave circuit.
Reference to the waveforms should enable pupils to offer a possible
reason. Careful questioning should produce the explanation that
each peak of the wave form represents a voltage 'pulse' which gives
the motor a 'push', or, better still, each pulse supplies energy to
the motor. Since there are twice as many pulses per second using
full-wave (100) than when using half-wave (50) rectification, the
motor speed changes - i.e. the average voltage supplied from a full-
wave circuit is higher than the average voltage from a half-wave
circuit.

In order to assist pupils in understanding the function of the extra
diodes used in full-wave circuits, they should observe the waveforms indicated across each half of the secondary of the transformer
as used in the two-diode circuit. The success of this test will
depend upon the type of oscilloscope available. Some success is
achieved if synchronisation is removed from the oscilloscope and
the trace made as near stationary as possible by means of the fine
velocity control. Each half of the transformer is then quickly
tested in turn.

Better still, arrange a switching circuit, using a d.p.d.t. switch
unit, to connect each end of the transformer in turn to the
oscilloscope Y input. The centre of the winding of the secondary
is connected to the 'earth' (common) terminal. By rapid switching,
the difference between the two traces is evident.

When correctly set up, the waveforms should appear 180° 'out of phase':

1st observation   2nd observation

A better result is achieved using a double-beam oscilloscope, enabling the two traces to be viewed simultaneously.

In 7, the turntable is 'loaded' either by adding a suitable weight to the turntable or more simply by 'braking' the turntable at its rim. Pupils should note the increase in the reading of current to the motor - an important fact in connection with the next assignment.

Apparatus Required (15 pupils, 5 groups of 3)

five transformer units

twenty diode units

five 50 ohm resistor units (5W)

five oscilloscopes

five turntable units - assembled

five 0-1 A ammeters

five suitable methods of loading the turntable motor, e.g. large weights (adding friction by means of a finger also works well)

<u>Note</u>: Investigation 6 is best performed using a double-beam oscilloscope, in order to observe the two waveforms simultaneously.

Demonstration

Demonstrate the use of a double-beam oscilloscope in order that the waveforms at each end of the transformer secondary can be seen simultaneously.

Homework Questions

1 Illustrate two major differences between full-wave 'bridge' rectification and full-wave rectification.

Modern miniaturised electronic equipment usually employs the 'bridge' rectification circuit. Why do you think this is?

2 Design a battery charger circuit, with the following features:

a) a means of measuring the charging current,

b) a control to vary the charging current,

c) a pilot lamp to indicate that the unit is switched on,

d) an on-off switch,

e) a means of cutting off the supply from the battery if the battery being charged suddenly develops a short-circuit.

3 Design a power supply to give outputs of 6 volts d.c. and 24 volts d.c. from the same transformer.

4 One of the diodes becomes faulty in a full-wave rectifier circuit. What will the effect be if:

a) the diode goes short-circuit?

b) the diode goes open-circuit?

RECTIFICATION ASSIGNMENT 3

For most applications, mains-derived d.c. power supplies should be 'smooth'. This is particularly important when the supply is used to power an electronic circuit. A smooth supply, approximating to the d.c. provided by primary cells (e.g. torch cells) or secondary (rechargeable) cells (e.g. the motor-car accumulator) is often essential. The d.c. obtained by pupils in the previous assignments is far from smooth, being in the form of pulses.

Graphical representations of 'smooth' and 'pulsed' d.c.

The purpose of assignment 3 is to attempt to produce smooth d.c. supplies by fitting 'smoothing capacitors', and to discover the factors which determine the value of the capacitor required. Pupils will discover that, for a given value of smoothing capacitor, the

175

larger the current taken from the supply, the greater is the ripple.
The optimum value selected for a particular purpose is determined
by the current consumed and the allowable ripple content of the d.c.
output.

Apparatus Required (15 pupils, 5 groups of 3)

twenty diode units

five transformer units

five 5000μF capacitors (any value in this region)

five 1000μF capacitors (or values in this region)

various capacitors, ranging from 100μF to 10 000 F

five oscilloscopes

five 50 ohm resistor units (5W) } these, in series and parallel,
ten 25 ohm resistor units (5W) } will provide alternative values
of resistance in 3

stackable 4mm plug leads - assorted lengths

various capacitors, ranging from 100 μF to 10 000 μF

Demonstrations

1   If possible, show the layout and components of a power supply
    incorporated in a piece of electronic equipment.

2   By group discussion and demonstration, summarise the Rectifica-
    tion assignments.

Homework Questions

1   Draw sketch graphs to represent the output from an unsmoothed
    rectified supply and from a battery used in a torch.   Explain
    the differences between the two graphs.

2   The value of the output voltage from an unsmoothed rectification
    circuit, as measured on a voltmeter, is different from that of
    a similar circuit incorporating a smoothing capacitor.   Why do
    these voltages differ?

3   Two separate power supplies, each consisting of a transformer
    and a full-wave rectifier, supply 3 amperes at 12 volts to
    external circuitry.   If a 'smooth' output is essential, which
    will require the smallest smoothing capacitor, assuming one
    operates from 250 volts, 50 Hz and the other from 250 volts,
    500 Hz?

4   'The greater the current taken from a smoothed rectification
    circuit, the greater is the ripple content of the output.' Give
    an explanation for this effect.

THE TRANSISTOR

Pupils have already become acquainted with one semiconductor device, the semiconductor diode, and they are now introduced to a second, more versatile, one: the transistor. As a result of this series of assignments, pupils become familiar with some of the more important properties of the transistor. Assignment 5 asks pupils to modify an existing circuit to produce a light-operated switch incorporating a transistor. Having successfully completed the investigation, pupils have a practical circuit suitable for use in later project work. It is anticipated that, when all five assignments have been completed, teachers will introduce pupils to more complex circuitry, and perhaps discuss alternative methods of assembly.

TRANSISTOR ASSIGNMENT 1

Here pupils examine a transistor unit containing a power transistor, and names are given to the three connections. The teacher should have several different types of transistor available for the pupils to examine. It should be emphasised that the transistor itself is usually much smaller than its package suggests. It is possible to remove the top from a type contained in a metal can in order to make the construction visible. A binocular microscope is perhaps necessary. Some transistors encapsulated in a metal case are coated in silicon grease, which is rather difficult to remove completely.

The three parts of the transistor - base, collector, and emitter - are easily identified in 'alloy' constructions.

The diagram shows the construction. Note the size of the collector region compared with the emitter. It is recommended that teachers should refer to suitable literature on transistor construction and manufacture, for background information.

Using the power transistor, pupils investigate the following:

1   The resistances measured between the base and emitter and between the collector and base. The measurements are repeated with the ohmmeter leads reversed. From their previous knowledge of diode action, pupils will note that a transistor in some

respects resembles two diodes 'back-to-back'. This information
provides a useful means of testing a transistor which is suspected of having been damaged by misuse. (It is assumed that
a transistor tester is not available.)

2   The effect of omitting a base connection when a lamp is fitted
in the collector circuit. The lamp will normally remain unillu-
minated, suggesting that either no current is passing between
collector and emitter or else a current which is insufficient
to light the lamp. In this instance, the latter becomes evident
- as pupils should note when making investigation 2 in Assignment 3.

3   The effect on the emitter-collector current when a base current
flows. In 6, a base current is provided by means of a 1.5 volt
cell. Pupils will note that the lamp in the collector circuit
is illuminated, whereas the lamp in the base circuit remains
unlit. This suggests that the base current is considerably less
than the collector current. This is confirmed when ammeters
are fitted in the base and collector circuits. Reversing the
1.5 volt cell prevents the lighting of the lamp in the collector
circuit. This emphasises the importance of connecting the base
supply voltage such that the base is positive with respect to
the emitter when using the npn-type transistor.

Apparatus Required (15 pupils, 5 groups of 3)

five power-transistor units

assorted transistors for demonstration, including other power and
small signal types

five ohmmeters

five diode units

ten lamp indicator units

five 1.5V cells

five power supplies - 12V d.c., 5A - with safety fuse or trip

five manual switch units

five multimeters or five 0-0.5A ammeters

stackable 4mm plug leads assorted lengths

Demonstration

Show a number of transistors, including both high- and low-power
types illustrating that pnp and npn types may look identical. Discuss
how to use an ohmmeter in order to determine whether a transistor
is npn or pnp. Refer to the diagram in Follow-up 1, part 3, during
the discussion.

Homework Questions

1   High-power diodes and transistors are often mounted on 'heat
sinks'. What is the purpose of a heat sink, and what is the
best material to use for the purpose?

2   You are given two unmarked transistors; one is known to be a
npn type and the other pnp. What test would you use to discover which is which?

3   In Transistor Follow-up 1 it is suggested that a power transistor can be likened to a relay, in that both can act as
switches. Suggest one advantage in using a transistor rather
than a relay. Give reasons.

4   In circuit diagrams, how are npn transistors distinguished from
pnp types?

TRANSISTOR ASSIGNMENT 2

A variable resistor is fitted into the base circuit of the transistor, in addition to the 1.5 volt cell. A lamp fitted in the
collector-emitter circuit varies its brightness as the variable
resistor is adjusted - diagram (a). In order to dispense with one
of the supplies (the 1.5 volt cell), the base current is then provided from the same supply as that feeding the collector - diagram
(b) below.

(a)   (b)

It must be stressed that if the fixed resistor R_2 is omitted, then
damage to the transistor may result. Should the variable resistor
be set to zero, in the absence of R_2, the 12 volt supply will be
connected directly across the base and emitter of the transistor.
This situation may damage the base-emitter region or, alternatively,
a large collector-emitter current may be produced which will cause
the transistor to overheat. Should the power transistors become
damaged despite warnings, the following modifications to the transistor unit are recommended:

a) Fit a 50 ohm, 5 watt wire-wound resistor between the green
    socket and the base of the transistor. This will afford con-
    siderable protection.

b) Fit a 5 ohm, 5 watt wire-wound resistor between the red socket
    and the transistor collector. (Ideally this resistor should be
    of about 30 watt rating to meet all conditions, but such a
    resistor would be too large to be fitted in the unit.) This
    resistor will afford some protection, but it or the transistor
    may still overheat if large collector currents are allowed over
    long periods of time.

Pupils replace the variable resistor by a photocell and are asked
to use the transistor first as a switch and then as a variable resistor. In the first instance, either full or no photocell illumination is required. This will result in the transistor passing either
a high current or almost none. In the second case, the transistor
acts rather like a variable resistor - in the sense that the current
between collector and emitter can be varied. The transistor
collector-emitter variations can be produced by varying the intensity of the illumination of the photocell by a suitable means.

Apparatus Required (15 pupils, 5 groups of 3)

five power supplies - 12V d.c., 5A - with safety fuse or trip

five power-transistor units

five 50 kilohm variable-resistor units

five 1.5 volt cells

five 50 ohm resistor units (5W)

five lamp indicator units

five 0-1A ammeters

five turntable units - assembled

five 50 ohm variable-resistor units - or 100 ohm (high wattage)

five photocell units

five light-source units

stackable 4mm plug leads - assorted lengths

Demonstration

Remove the outer casing from a small transistor in order that
pupils can identify the base, emitter, and collector regions under
a microscope (preferably binocular).

Homework Questions

1   What is the purpose of the 50 ohm resistor in the circuit shown below?

2   With reference to the circuit in question 1, if the lamp glows normally, what current is flowing in the collector circuit of the transistor?

3   A base current of 20 microamperes is found to produce a collector current of 1 milliampere. What is the current gain (H_{FE}) of the transistor at this collector current?

4   A 0.1A lamp fitted in the collector circuit of a transistor is to be illuminated fully when the transistor is conducting. If the current gain of the transistor is 100, what current must flow in the base circuit?

TRANSISTOR ASSIGNMENT 3

The purpose of this assignment is twofold:

a)   To indicate that there is always a small 'leakage' current between the collector and emitter of a transistor. This 'leakage' results in a small collector current even when the base current is zero. In many applications this small current is not important, but in others steps must be taken to reduce it,

b)   To determine the current gain of a transistor.

The leakage current, with the base open-circuited, is measured with a lamp included in the collector circuit. The purpose of the lamp is to protect the transistor should a large collector current be allowed to flow when the 1.5 volt cell is included in the base circuit (Transistor Assignment 3, part 2). It is probable that on some occasions the cell will be wrongly connected, with its positive terminal to the base of the transistor, rather than its negative terminal.

Leakage currents can be detrimental to the operation of some circuits, and pupils will appreciate this when they attempt to de-energise a relay fitted in place of a lamp. Lamp dimming is possible, but the relay fails to de-energise even when the base supply is removed, there often being sufficient leakage current in the collector circuit to maintain the relay in its energised condition. Pupils should be encouraged to try different ways of modifying the circuit in an attempt to cause the relay to both energise and de-energise, having first determined that they have a reasonable explanation for the failure of the circuit. The Follow-up describes one way of overcoming the difficulty, i.e. it indicates a method of completely 'shutting off' the transistor.

Current gain is explained in the follow-up. It should be noted that in transistor literature three symbols are in common usage for this quantity: the preferred symbol is H_{FE}, though α' (alpha dashed) or β (beta) have been used in the past.

Apparatus Required (15 pupils, 5 groups of 3)

five 0-1A ammeters

five 0-10 mA meters } or similar ranges
five 0-1 mA meters }

five power supplies - 12V d.c., 5A - with safety fuse or trip

five power-transistor units

five 50 kilohm variable-resistor units

five 50 ohm resistor units (5W)

five lamp indicator units

five 1.5 volt cells

five relay units

stackable 4mm plug leads - assorted lengths

Demonstration

Set up the transistor tester shown below in order to test the current gain of an assortment of transistors. It will also determine whether or not a transistor is faulty.

In order to test pnp transistors, the batteries and meters must be reversed. It is recommended that the circuit is wired up permanently in a suitable case, enabling pupils to test a transistor quickly, without the necessity of setting up the arrangement each time. In a permanent unit, an on-off switch should isolate one lead from each battery. Three terminal posts should be provided to make good electrical contact with the transistor leads, and ideally a change-over switch should be incorporated to reverse the meter and battery connections for testing both npn and pnp transistors.

Homework Questions

1   In the circuit diagram below, what is the purpose of R_2 and of B_2? If R_2 is omitted, why is the relay unlikely to de-energise when the variable resistor (R_1) is adjusted?

2   A circuit identical to that in question 1 is set up and it is found that the relay does not change over to the energised condition in any position of the variable resistor. Give <u>four</u> possible component failures (other than wiring) which could produce this result. Suggest a reason in each case.

3   A wire-wound variable resistor is suspected of being faulty. How would you test it in order to pronounce it 'serviceable' or 'unserviceable'?

4   Describe the behaviour of the lamp in the circuit below when the switch S is closed. Give reasons for your answers.

TRANSISTOR ASSIGNMENT 4

Pupils try out a potential-divider arrangement making use of two separate power supplies. This is to enable the relay in the collector circuit to energise and to de-energise by adjusting a variable

183

resistor in the transistor base circuit. Too small a value of
resistance from the supply B to the base (see the diagram on
Transistor Assignment 4, part 1) should not be used. A low resistance in the potential-divider network will result in overheating
of either the variable or the fixed resistor, especially when the
variable has a low resistance value. Note also that 24 volts is
applied across the potential-divider network.

By using 1.5 volt cells in a cell-carrier unit, pupils are able to
determine whether the voltage on the transistor base must be positive, negative, or zero with respect to its emitter. In addition,
they use a current meter to find the minimum energising current and
the minimum hold-on current for the relay they are using. The
teacher should ensure that all pupils can give an explanation for
the difference between these two values.

Apparatus Required (15 pupils, 5 groups of 3)

five power-supply units: 6-12V d.c. low current only required, e.g.
cell-carrier units

five power supplies - 12V, 5A - with safety fuse or trip

five power-transistor units

five lamp indicator units

five 10 kilohm resistor units ($\frac{1}{4}$W)

five 50 kilohm resistor units (5W)

assorted values of $\frac{1}{4}$W resistors from 2 kilohm to about 100 kilohm.

five fuse-carrier units - for mounting various values of resistor

five 0-10V voltmeters

five relay units

five 0-100 mA meters

stackable 4mm plug leads - assorted lengths

Demonstrations

Teachers may wish to
demonstrate the
following circuits
to the more able
pupils.

Pupils will note that the lamp illuminates when light is incident upon the photocell. Replace the lamp by a 50 ohm resistor unit, and fit a suitable voltmeter, say 0-20 volt but of high resistance, in the position shown.

Note that when the photocell is illuminated the reading on the voltmeter is small, i.e. the collector voltage is low; and when no light strikes the photocell, the voltage at the collector is high. Now feed this voltage, through a 10 kilohm current-limiting resistor, to a second stage - a lamp being placed in the collector circuit of the second transistor.

When the photocell is illuminated, the lamp remains extinguished in this new arrangement but glows when light is prevented from reaching the photocell. Thus the second stage behaves as an inverter. Inversion by this technique is frequently employed in logic circuitry.

Homework Questions

1   In general, electromagnetic relays require a greater current to cause them to 'energise' than to keep them 'energised'. Suggest one reason for this.

2   In the circuit shown below, obstruction A prevents light from
    reaching the photocell.

    a)   What happens to the motor when the switch S is closed and
         the obstruction is removed?

    b)   What is the most probable effect on the motor when the
         obstruction is replaced?

3   The current gain of the transistor in the circuit shown below
    is 100. Assuming that the base to emitter resistance is zero,

    a)   how much base (base-emitter) current flows in the trans-
         istor?

    b)   how much collector (collector-emitter) current flows in
         the transistor?

    c)   what power rating would you use for the 100 ohm resistor:
         1, 2, 3, 4, 5, or 6 watts?

    Show clearly how you arrived at each of your answers.

4   When the switch S is closed in the circuit shown below, the
    lamp glows only dimly. Suggest two possible ways of making the
    lamp glow with normal brilliance without changing the circuit
    arrangement.

TRANSISTOR ASSIGNMENT 5

A familiar circuit is presented to pupils and they are asked to
modify it. By using a photocell in the base circuit of the transistor, a very sensitive light-operated switch is produced, and
several investigations are suggested. By reversing the positions
of the photocell and the fixed resistor in the potential-divider
feeding the base circuit of the transistor, the operation of the
circuit becomes reversed. In the first case - the photocell
connected between supply positive and base - the relay is energised
when the cell is illuminated and de-energised when the light incident upon the cell is blocked. On reversing the two components the
relay is de-energised when light is incident upon the cell and
energised when the light is blocked.

Having completed this series of assignments on the transistor, and
having been introduced to a useful light-operated switch, investigations involving more advanced electronic circuits should be
feasible with the more able pupils. Control involving electronic
circuits will sooner or later lead to the necessity to use logic
circuitry. The elements of logic should, therefore, be studied at
this stage.

Apparatus Required (15 pupils, 5 groups of 3)

five lamp indicator units

five 50 ohm resistor units (5W)

five 50 kilohm resistor units

five 10 kilohm resistor units (¼W)

five power supplies - 12V, 5A - with safety fuse or trip

five cell-carrier units, or any 6-12V low-current d.c. supplies

five photocell units

five two-pole, two-way relay units

five turntable units - assembled

five power-transistor units

stackable 4mm plug leads - assorted lengths

Demonstration

Pupils will have already met two types of relay delay circuits - one
in Electrical-switching Assignment 5 and another suggested in the
teachers' notes for Electrical-switching Assignment 5. The latter
employs a variable resistor in series with a relay coil shunted by
a capacitor. If this circuit has not been demonstrated, teachers
may wish to do so now. A less critical transistor circuit is shown
below. Since it may enable pupils to be more versatile when dealing
with design problems, it is recommended that the teacher should
demonstrate the technique to pupils of suitable ability.

When switch S is closed, the current flowing in the variable resistor begins to charge up the capacitor in preference to causing a
base current to flow (an uncharged capacitor behaves as a short-
circuit). A base current begins to flow when the capacitor has
charged sufficiently, and hence a collector current flows. Eventually the collector current is high enough to energise the relay,
and the lamp illuminates. Increasing the resistance of the rheostat increases the delay time by decreasing the charging rate of
the capacitor.

Homework Questions

1   If you were to set up the following circuit, what effects would you expect if the light from one or both of the light sources were to be blocked?

2   When light strikes the photocell in the circuit shown below, what approximate voltage reading would you expect on the volt-meter? If the light were to be prevented from reaching the cell, what would you expect to happen to the voltmeter reading? (<u>Hint</u>: What is the resistance between the collector and emitter of a fully conducting transistor compared with a non-conducting transistor?)

3   In the following circuit, the diode in the supply line acts as a safety device. For what specific purpose is this diode likely to be included?

4   Redraw the following circuit for use with **a pnp** transistor.

190

Logic circuits

All the logic circuits investigated through the use of the d.p.d.t. switch boxes in the logic assignments can be arranged using other switching devices, e.g. pneumatic valves, turbulence amplifiers, and transistors.

PNEUMATIC LOGIC CIRCUITS

OR (AND/OR)

A shuttle valve gives a
two input OR facility

$A \lor B = Z$

To increase the number of inputs, connect more shuttle valves as shown.

Four-input OR arrangement

$A \& B \& C = Z$

<u>NOR</u>

This may be achieved by either of the following arrangements:

a)   (Inverting the output of an OR arrangement)

$$\overline{A \vee B} = Z$$

b)

$$\overline{A \vee B \vee C} = Z$$

<u>NAND</u>

The simplest method is to invert the output of an AND arrangement:

$$\overline{A \& B \& C} = Z$$

<u>Note</u>: Teachers may prefer to use Boolean logic notation, whereby
A AND B is written A.B; A OR B is written A + B

LOGIC CIRCUITS USING TURBULENCE AMPLIFIERS

<u>NOR</u>

The turbulence amplifier is a NOR unit.

$$\overline{A \vee B \vee C \vee D} = Z$$

Output Z is obtained only if neither input A nor B nor C nor D is present.

<u>OR</u>

$$A \vee B \vee C \vee D = Z$$

If an input is applied at either A, B, C or D, turbulence amplifier 1 will give no output and, therefore, turbulence amplifier 2 will give an output.

<u>AND</u>

$$A \& B = Z$$

There is an output Z only if both A and B are present.

NAND

A&B&C=Z

An output Z is obtained unless all input signals A,B, and C are present.

ELECTRONIC LOGIC CIRCUITS

For detailed information concerning the various electronic logic circuits suitable for work in schools, teachers should refer to the Project Technology Handbook No.14, Simple Computer and Control Logic, published by Heinemann Educational Ltd.   This handbook provides guidance for teachers who wish to involve pupils in practical applications of various aspects of computer and control logic.

THE APPROACH TO LOGIC PROBLEMS

By adopting a planned approach, as indicated in the following example, it is possible to solve most logic problems.

Procedure

1   State the problem in words.

2   Write out the logic equation.

3   Draw in block-diagram form.

4   Construct a truth table.

5   Draw the circuit diagram.

194

1   Problem

Devise a system which will enable a metal press to be operated
when a manual switch A, or a manual switch B, and guard-posi-
tion sensor C are depressed, but not if switch D, which
indicates that the previous component has not been removed, is
activated.

This may also be written:

Devise a system which will enable a metal press to be operated
if either manual switch A or manual switch B is depressed and
the guard sensing switch is operated and not if the previous
component indicator switch D is activated.

2   $A \vee B \mathbin{\&} C \mathbin{\&} \bar{D} = Z$

3

4

A	B	C	D	$A \vee B$	$\bar{D}$	$C \mathbin{\&} \bar{D}$	$A \vee B \mathbin{\&} C \mathbin{\&} \bar{D}$	
0	0	0	0	0	1	0	0	
0	0	0	1	0	0	0	0	
0	0	1	0	0	1	1	0	
0	0	1	1	0	0	0	0	
0	1	0	0	1	1	0	0	
0	1	0	1	1	0	0	0	
0	1	1	0	1	1	1	1	- operation
0	1	1	1	1	0	0	0	
1	0	0	0	1	1	0	0	
1	0	0	1	1	0	0	0	
1	0	1	0	1	1	1	1	- operation
1	0	1	1	1	0	0	0	
1	1	0	0	1	1	0	0	
1	1	0	1	1	0	0	0	
1	1	1	0	1	1	1	1	- operation
1	1	1	1	1	0	0	0	

5 An electrical circuit diagram representing this logic equation can be drawn:

This can also be achieved using manual switches only:

A similar, and perhaps more appropriate, circuit for this particular problem could be assembled using other switching devices, e.g. pneumatic valves.

Circuit using three logic gates as indicated in the block diagram:

To reduce the number of components required, this can be achieved using only mechanically operated valves:

SOME FURTHER PRACTICAL WORK FOR PUPILS

1   Using three or more electrical switches (pneumatic valves, etc),
    arrange them in various ways to produce logic circuits, such as:

e.g.

When a switch is open call it "0"; and when it is closed call
it "1". If the lamp illuminates call the result "1"; and if it
fails to illuminate call the result "0".

Draw up a truth table headed as shown below and complete it for
all the possible switch arrangements.

A	B	C	(D)	result

From the truth table, establish the logic arrangement.

2   If much emphasis is to be placed on logic circuits, it may
    prove worthwhile to construct a demonstration board using the
    electronic circuits.

    Suggested layout for demonstration board (all sockets 4mm)

198

Although designed for the teacher's use when demonstrating logic circuitry, this also allows pupils to test their solutions to logic problems very easily and quickly. The same piece of equipment can be used to operate models, since relays can be driven through the amplifier sockets.

LOGIC PROBLEMS

1   In a bank, a large number of mixed coins, halfpennies, pennies, two-pence, five-pence, ten-pence, and fifty-pence pieces are to be sorted into a box containing only silver coins and a box containing only copper coins. The mixed coins are fed into a chute and arrive at a fast-acting gate with a separation of about 100mm between them. Produce a block logic diagram, a truth table, and a logic equation which will enable the gate to direct the coins into their appropriate boxes. The sensors fitted detect the size of the coin (not whether copper or silver).

2   Produce a suitable logic system, consisting of a logic equation, a block logic diagram, and a truth table, to control a metal-drilling machine. Sensors are fitted to detect that a piece of work is in position and that the safety guard is down. Two on-off switches are provided – one at each end of the machine – either of which will switch on the drilling mechanism if the work is in place and the guard is down.

3   A sorting maching is supplied with components of various widths, of which some are too wide and some too narrow. It is required to extract those of acceptable width. Produce a logical equation, a block logic diagram, and a truth table; and suggest a suitable circuit.

4   The diagram below shows an intersection of two one-way streets The symbols X represent traffic lights consisting of red and green lights only. Design a control system which will operate the traffic lights. The vehicle arriving at the junction first must be given priority, but if two vehicles (one at A and one at B) arrive simultaneously then both must stop. When two vehicles are waiting, B is to be given priority to move off first.

A possible group project

This project based on the turntable unit can be tried either after
the Transistor assignments or immediately following a short course
on logic and logic circuitry. Although some teachers will no doubt
have made use of the turntable as part of other projects from time
to time (involving different solutions by the various groups in a
class), this project is intended to involve all pupils in a class
of about fifteen. Each group of three or four pupils might be
concerned directly with some aspect of the problem. When all groups
have perfected their particular solution, all the various parts are
brought together to produce a working device. The theme of this
project, and the possible solution offered here, is intended only
as a guide in order that teachers and pupils will be encouraged to
suggest and solve problems along similar lines, usually working as
a group. Whilst some teachers may wish to involve pupils in
solving the problem specified here, the solution offered is given
primarily as a means of showing how the project might be developed;
it is certainly not the only solution, and undoubtedly not the best,
though teachers might wish to make use of some of the ideas in one
way or another with pupils of high ability.

DEFINITION OF THE PROBLEM

The project is concerned with the building of a device which can
'recognise', and thereafter indicate the recognition of, the height
and diameter of cylindrically shaped objects placed upon the turntable. Four cylinders are requied: 75mm x 25mm dia., 75mm x 18mm
dia., 50mm x 25mm dia., and 50mm x 18mm dia. Since these are to be
placed upright on the moving turntable, mild steel is a suitable
material. The weight of each is sufficient to ensure that they
remain in the upright position. Less dense materials are more
likely to 'topple' should there be any jerky notion of the turntable.

The design of the circuitry for the control of the turntable and the
recognition of the articles placed upon it should be such that any
of the four objects can be identified individually, or any combination indicated.

Since there are four different items, there are sixteen possible
arrangements which can be accepted (or rejected) by the device. The
arrangements which could be indicated as 'accepted' are:

1   none of them,
2   long and fat,
3   short and fat,
4   either short and fat or long and fat,

5 long and thin,
6 either long and thin or long and fat,
7 either long and thin or short and fat,
8 long and thin, short and fat, or long and fat (i.e. not short and thin),
9 short and thin,
10 either short and thin or long and fat,
11 either short and thin or short and fat,
12 short and thin, short and fat, or long and fat (i.e. not long and thin),
13 either short and thin or long and thin,
14 short and thin, long and thin, or long and fat (i.e. not short and fat),
15 short and thin, long and thin, or short and fat (i.e. not long and fat),
16 all of them.

For simplicity, 'long' refers to a 75mm piece, 'short' to a 50mm piece; 'thin' to a 18mm dia. piece, and 'fat' to a 25mm piece. In the solution offered, acceptance of any piece is indicated by the illumination of a lamp. For instance, if the device is 'set' for condition 12, the lamp will illuminate if a short and thin, short and fat, or long and fat cylinder is detected, but it will remain extinguished if a long and thin cylinder is detected. The versatility required from the device should now be evident, in that one must be able to 'program' it in any one of sixteen different ways. Teachers familiar with the principles of logic will no doubt recognise that here we have a logic problem. This does not necessarily mean, however, that pupils (or teachers) should have some knowledge of logic before attempting such a project; indeed, having found a solution which works, the advantage of a logical study of the problem becomes self-evident. A short course in logic followed by a reappraisal of the problem in logic terms could prove stimulating to the more able pupil.

WORK DISTRIBUTION

The problem as a whole can be conveniently divided into four parts, a group of, say, three pupils being responsible for each part. However, some coordination between groups is essential, since eventually each of the four parts must fit together to form a whole. Thus one group of three pupils could be responsible for this coordination and would probably need to spend quite a lot of their time working with all groups in some sort of sequence. A typical distribution could be:

a) a means of detecting height - short or long;
b) a means of detecting width - fat or thin;
c) a means of starting the turntable manually when a specimen has been placed upon the turntable, and a means of stopping it automatically after exactly one turntable revolution;

d) determining the number of possibilities and devising an 'accept' or 'reject' circuit when a cylinder is sensed;

e) coordination between the four groups.

Indication of 'accept' - say, lamp illuminated - and 'reject' - say, lamp remains extinguished - is probably best arranged to occur at the end of the cycle when the turntable stops.

A POSSIBLE SOLUTION

This solution is based entirely on the basic units designed specially for the course. Height and width are detected using photocells and associated light sources, the photocells being mounted at the periphery of the turntable unit and the light sources at the centre. In order to do this, a gantry spanning the unit is required; the light sources are then attached to a vertical dropped from the centre of the gantry. The 'accept' or 'reject' indicator lamp is also placed on the gantry. Connecting leads for the indicator and light sources should be attached to the gantry to prevent any obstruction of the cylinders as they rotate on the turntable.

Fig.1

indicator lamp

light sources

Meccano gantry made from angle

photocells

microswitch unit operated by bolt located in the edge of the turntable

A hole is drilled into the edge of the turntable proper; the hole is tapped M3; and a screw is part-way inserted and locked in position with a nut. This screw operates a microswitch attached to one of the existing Meccano brackets which space the top and bottom square Perspex turntable plates.

Fig.2

Control Unit and Turntable-Motor Control

Control of the turntable motor is achieved through a relay bistable unit. This unit is triggered either by the microswitch on the turn-table or by the manual push button circuit (control unit). The connections C, in conjunction with a power supply, two sets of switch contacts (A and B) and a lamp indicator unit, enable any of the sixteen different arrangements to be selected. The wiring between points S is dealt with later. In addition to triggering the bistable unit, the control unit receives and sends information to the height-detection and width-detection units. This information is carried through connections W, X, and Y. When the manual push button on the control unit is pressed momentarily, the short-circuit across the terminals 1 and 2 on the bistable unit causes it to change over; the turntable motor starts to run; and a short-circuit appears across the connections C, when it eventually stops. Because of the latter occurrence, the indicator on the gantry illuminates under the correct conditions only at the end of a cycle. Note that the manual push button must be pressed for a sufficient time to allow the bolt-head to break contact with the microswitch situated at the periphery of the turntable.

Fig.3

lamp indicator

switches A and B in RL3 and RL2

12 V

(connection)

turntable motor

TURNTABLE MOTOR CONTROL UNIT

bistable relays

microswitch on turntable

12 V

CONTROL UNIT

Y
Y
X
X
W
W

4 pole, 2 way relay unit

12 V

manual push-button switch

<u>Note</u>: In this and all other circuits relating to the project, separate power supplies are shown in each unit, to preserve clarity. In practice, only one is necessary.

Height Detection

Fig 4

HEIGHT UNIT

photocell

12 V

RL3

Y

Y

A

The height detector makes use of the photocell uppermost on the gantry, in conjunction with a two-pole, two-way relay unit. Since the photocell is normally illuminated - only a long specimen prevents light striking this cell - the relay will be normally energised. Because of the circuit arrangement, however, the relay can energise only if the connections Y are short-circuited, this occurring briefly when the manual push button on the control unit is operated. If a long specimen prevents light striking the photo-cell, the relay de-energises and remains de-energised until the start of the next test, when the manual push button on the control unit is again depressed. Thus the device 'remembers' it has just sensed a long specimen. Alternatively, if the photocell receives light throughout the whole cycle, it 'remembers' that either the specimen was short or that there was no specimen present. The set of switch contacts marked A, mentioned previously under 'Control unit and turntable-motor control', will be dealt with later.

Width Detection

Width detection is described using two different techniques; the first uses a transistor circuit and the second a simpler arrange-ment similar to the height-detection unit. Although it is more involved, the transistor design is more reliable than the simpler relay circuit, and it is more easily adjusted. The bottom photo-cell is used for width detection. Both long and short specimens are arranged to block the light reaching the photocell, but obviously a fat (large diameter) specimen will block the light to the cell for a longer time than a thin one. Both detection methods are based upon this difference in time.

Width Unit Transistor Arrangement

RL_1 is always energised when light is incident upon the photocell, and under this condition the base circuit (50kilohm variable) of the transistor is disconnected from the power supply and is inoper-ative. When any specimen, thin or fat, breaks the beam to the

Fig.5

WIDTH UNIT

photocell, RL_1 immediately de-energises and supply is fed to the transistor base. The transistor does not immediately conduct, however, since a large value capacitor (2500μF approx.) is connected between the base and emitter. This capacitor is initially uncharged and behaves like a short-circuit; thus, instead of current flowing to the transistor base, it charges the capacitor. As the capacitor charges, its effective resistance gradually increases and an increasing base current begins to flow. Initially RL2 is energised, it is connected to the supply through the 50 ohm resistor, and the transistor is not conducting.

As the transistor begins to conduct, however, its falling resistance causes the voltage across the transistor to fall. This voltage is also across the relay coil (since they are both in parallel) and, if the photocell remains non-illuminated for a long period (fat speci-men), the voltage across the relay falls to too low a value to keep it energised. It therefore changes over to the de-energised state until the contacts W are short-circuited by the manual push button; thus the device 'remembers' that a fat specimen has been detected. A thin specimen breaks the light to the photocell for a shorter duration, and the current in the transistor does not reach a suffi-ciently high value to cause the relay RL2 to de-energise. Obviously critical adjustment is necessary, and this is achieved through the 50kilohm variable resistance which changes the rate at which the capacitor can charge. If the relay RL2 de-energises even when a thin specimen passes, then the resistance of the variable resistor must be increased to cause a longer delay. The contacts B have been mentioned previously under 'Control unit and turntable-control motor', and will be dealt with later.

Width Unit, Simple Arrangement:

Fig 6

This relay circuit is only one of a number of possibilities. RL1 is energised whenever light is incident upon the photocell. When the beam is broken, supply is fed to RL2 through the 100 ohm variable resistor. However, RL2 does not immediately energise owing to the uncharged capacitor C (5000μF approx.). This capacitor behaves as a very low resistance in its uncharged state, causing the bulk of the current to by-pass the relay coil. As the capacitor charges, a greater proportion of the current flows in the relay coil until there is sufficient to energise it. The delay time is determined by the setting of the variable resistor - the greater the resistance, the slower the charging rate. It should be noted, however, that there is likely to be a setting beyond which the relay will never energise, too large a resistance limiting the maximum current to a value which is too small to energise the relay - even when the capacitor has fully charged. Adjust the variable resistor until RL2 energises for a fat specimen but not for a thin.

If RL2 energises, the normally energised RL3 de-energises and remains de-energised irrespective of any subsequent state of RL2. Thus the circuit 'remembers' if a fat specimen has been detected. Contacts B are dealt with later.

Fig.7 Complete Circuit of the Device

Selection of Function (programming)

As mentioned previously, the selection of any of the sixteen
possible arrangements is achieved by suitably wiring the two
connections S, a power supply, the indicator lamp on the gantry,
the switch contacts A in the height-detection unit and the switch
connections B in the width-detection unit. The switching arrangement necessary for any particular function is inserted between
points S in the common circuit of fig.8. The wiring of switches
A and B for each function is shown in table 1.

Fig.8

from
bistable

Table (1)

Selection	Arrangement of A and B between S-S
1 None	
2 Long and fat	
3 Short and fat	
4 Either short and fat or long and fat	
5 Long and thin	
6 Either long and thin or long and fat	
7 Either long and thin or short and fat	
8 Long and thin Short and fat Long and fat	
9 Short and thin	
10 Either short and thin or long and fat	

11 Either short and thin
   or short and fat

12 Short and thin
   Short and fat
   Long and fat

13 Either short and thin
   or long and thin

14 Short and thin
   Long and thin
   Long and fat

15 Short and thin
   Long and thin
   Short and fat

16 All

Note that the position shown for switches A and B are those prior to sensing.

Example:

height-circuit relay   RL2 width circuit

211

TESTING

1 Test each unit separately and to ensure that it operates
correctly, simulate the working conditions. Temporarily
connect a lamp and power supply to each of the contacts A and
B in order to determine the states of the relays during testing.

Height Unit

Switch on the supply. The relay should not energise. Short
together the Y connections and the relay should energise; if
not, check that light is striking the photocell. If the relay
energises, break the beam to the photocell and the relay should
de-energise and remain de-energised. Again, short together the
connections Y and the relay should energise. This completes
the testing of the height unit.

Width Unit - Transistor Type

Turn the 50 kilohm variable resistor to minimum resistance.
Switch on the supply. Both relays should immediately energise.
If the photocell relay (RL1 - complete circuit diagram) does
not energise, check that light is striking the photocell. If
RL1 energises but RL2 does not, check the transistor-circuit
wiring. If both relays energise, break the beam of light to
the photocell and both relays should de-energise. Allow light
to strike the cell again; RL1 should immediately energise and
RL2 should remain de-energised. Short-circuit the connections
W, and RL2 should again energise.

Rotate the 50kilohm variable resistor about ¼ turn. Break
the light beam to the photocell momentarily. RL1 should de-
energise but RL2 should remain energised. Now break the beam
for a much longer time and both relays should de-energise.
Short together both connections W and connections X, and RL2
should again energise. This completes the testing of the width
unit.

Control Unit

This simple unit should give no problems. Switch on the supply
and push the manual push button switch. The relay should
energise when the switch is depressed and de-energise when the
switch is released.

Motor-Control Unit

Connect a lamp and a power supply in series with the connections
C. Alternately shorting out the terminals marked 1 and 2 and
operating a microswitch fitted across the other pair of input
terminals should cause the bistable to change state.

2   Interconnect each unit. Wire in the turntable microswitch and
     motor. Press the manual push button and the turntable should
     rotate 1 revolution, stopping again when the turntable micro-
     switch is operated by the rotating turntable. Wire up
     connections C in series with the power supply and the indicator
     lamp on the gantry. This should leave two flying leads S.
     Connect one of these leads to the pole of relay switch contacts
     A on the height unit and the other to the normally open (rear)
     contact. Place a tall specimen on the turntable. Press the
     manual push button, allowing the turntable to rotate one revo-
     lution. When it stops, the indicator should illuminate, showing
     that it has recognised a tall object. Repeat for a short
     specimen and the lamp should not illuminate.

     Remove the flying leads S from relay contacts A on the height
     unit and wire them similarly to the relay contacts B on the
     width unit. Place the short and thin specimen on the turntable
     and press the manual push button switch. When the revolution
     is complete, the indicator lamp should remain extinguished.
     Repeat for the short and fat specimen and the lamp should
     illuminate. Find a setting of the 50kilohm variable resistor
     which causes the lamp to illuminate with a short and fat speci-
     men but not with a short and thin specimen. The testing is now
     complete. By suitable wiring of contacts A and B, as shown in
     table 1, any selection of specimens should be possible.

AN EXPLANATION USING THE RULES OF LOGIC

This section is intended for teachers who are familiar with logic
and logic circuitry. Some of these teachers may wish to discuss
the project after completion, along the following lines with the
more able pupils.

There are sixteen alternative selections when using four different
'characteristics' - four different 'characteristics' being short,
long, thin, and fat. Using binary notation, the sixteen are repre-
sented as shown in table 2.

TABLE 2

Note: '1' represents a selection; '0' represents no selection.

	Short thin	Short fat	Long thin	Long fat
Line 1	O	O	O	O
Line 2	O	O	O	1
Line 3	O	1	O	O
Line 4	O	1	O	1
Line 5	O	O	1	O

213

Line 6	0	0	1	1
Line 7	0	1	1	0
Line 8	0	1	1	1
Line 9	1	0	0	0
Line 10	1	0	0	1
Line 11	1	1	0	0
Line 12	1	1	0	1
Line 13	1	0	1	0
Line 14	1	0	1	1
Line 15	1	1	1	0
Line 16	1	1	1	1

The first line means that we must provide for the selection of none
of the specimens; the second long and fat; the fourth either short
and fat or long and fat; the eighth long and thin, short and fat,
or long and fat; and so on.

One can now write out truth tables for each 'line' in which the
switches A and B represent the 'inputs' of 1 or 0 (operated or not
operated) and each line represents the output column - note that
our horizontal lines now become vertical columns. The output
columns will be labelled Z (table 3). Alongside each truth table
is the logic equation in Boolean algebraic form, the selection which
causes the indicator lamp to illuminate, and the wiring of switches
A and B to give this selection. To simplify the description, short
and thin has been abbreviated to ST, long and thin to LT, short and
fat to SF, and long and fat to LF. The switching arrangement
necessary for any particular selection is inserted between points S
in fig.9.

Fig.9

from
bistable

indicator
lamp

Table 3

Line in table 2	Truth table			Logic equation	Selection	Wiring between S - S
	A	B	Z			
1) 0000					None	Omitted
ST	0	0	0			
SF	0	0	0			
LT	0	0	0			
LF	0	0	0			

214

2) 0001 A B Z $A \& B = Z$ Long and fat
   ST   0 0 0   (AND)
   SF   0 1 0
   LT   1 0 0
   LF   1 1 1

3) 0100 A B Z $B \& \bar{A} = Z$ Short and fat
   ST   0 0 0
   SF   0 1 1
   LT   1 0 0
   LF   1 1 0

4) 0101 A B Z $(A \& B) \lor B = Z$ Either short
   ST   0 0 0   and fat or
   SF   0 1 1   long and fat
   LT   1 0 0
   LF   1 1 1

5) 0010 A B Z $A \& \bar{B} = Z$ Long and thin
   ST   0 0 0
   SF   0 1 0
   LT   1 0 1
   LF   1 1 0

6) 0011 A B Z $(A \& B) \lor A = Z$ Either long
   ST   0 0 0   and thin or
   SF   0 1 0   long and fat
   LT   1 0 1
   LF   1 1 1

7) 0110 A B Z $A \lor B \& \overline{A \& B} = Z$ Either long
   ST   0 0 0   (Exclusive OR)   and thin or
   SF   0 1 1   short and
   LT   1 0 1   fat
   LF   1 1 0

8) 0111 A B Z $A \lor B = Z$ Long and
   ST   0 0 0   (OR)   thin, short
   SF   0 1 1   and fat,
   LT   1 0 1   long and fat
   LF   1 1 1

9) 1000 A B Z $\overline{A \lor B} = Z$ Short and
   ST   0 0 1   (NOR)   thin
   SF   0 1 0
   LT   1 0 0
   LF   1 1 0

10) 1001

	A	B	Z
ST	0	0	1
SF	0	1	0
LT	1	0	0
LF	1	1	1

$A \& B \lor \overline{A \lor B} = Z$
(Logical Equivalence)

Either short and thin or long and fat

11) 1100

	A	B	Z
ST	0	0	1
SF	0	1	1
LT	1	0	0
LF	1	1	0

$\overline{(A \& B) \lor A} = Z$

Either short and thin or short and fat

12) 1101

	A	B	Z
ST	0	0	1
SF	0	1	1
LT	1	0	0
LF	1	1	1

$B \lor \overline{A \lor B} = Z$

Short and thin, short and fat, long and fat

13) 1010

	A	B	Z
ST	0	0	1
SF	0	1	0
LT	1	0	1
LF	1	1	0

$\overline{(A \& B) \lor B} = Z$

Either short and thin or long and thin

14) 1011

	A	B	Z
ST	0	0	1
SF	0	1	0
LT	1	0	1
LF	1	1	1

$\overline{B} \& \overline{\overline{A}} = Z$

Short and thin, long and thin, long and fat

15) 1110

	A	B	Z
ST	0	0	1
SF	0	1	1
LT	1	0	1
LF	1	1	0

$\overline{A \& B} = Z$
(NAND)

Short and thin
Long and thin
Short and fat

16) 1111

	A	B	Z
ST	0	0	1
SF	0	1	1
LT	1	0	1
LF	1	1	1

$A \lor B \lor \overline{A \lor B} = Z$

All

Note: Teachers may prefer to use Boolean logic notation, whereby:

A AND B is written A.B
A OR B is written A + B

Appendix 1

PHOTOELASTIC STRESS ANALYSIS

The phenomenon of photoelasticity makes it possible to measure
stress and strain by detecting changes in the indexes of refraction
of light passing through the photoelastic material. The principle
is based on the fact that polarised light passing through a trans-
parent, birefringent plastics material under strain will split into
two polarised beams which travel in the planes of the principal
strains. These beams will have different velocities and therefore
different wavelengths, and the result is the production of a series
of coloured areas or lines. These are known as 'isochromatics', in
which areas of equal colour represent areas of equal stress. In
this range of colours, there is a distinct zone where the red is
immediately followed by a blue-green. This zone, which can easily
be located, is known as the 'tint of passage' or fringe boundary.

The polarising axes of the
polariser and analyser are
at right angles

polariser   analyser

Principle of
the simple
polariscope

light source   stressed model
of component
(made from
photoelastic
material)

If the material is stressed sufficiently, there will be more than
one complete sequence of colours, and several fringes will appear,
the number of fringes being a linear measure of the magnitude of
the stress.

Providing the polarisers used are large enough, the whole of the
model of the component can be examined. This ability to see the
complete stress field is one of the important advantages of the
photoelastic technique.

Principle of the polariscope

The design of a simple polariscope required for the photoelastic demonstrations can be based on the items shown here.

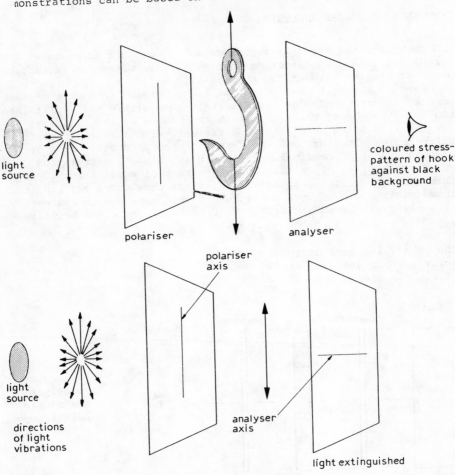

light source

polariser

polariser axis

analyser

coloured stress-pattern of hook against black background

light source

directions of light vibrations

analyser axis

light extinguished

To demonstrate the forces present in simple structures, it is often necessary to compare one design solution with another. It is very difficult to remember (or record by sketching) the pattern produced in one experiment and compare this with another produced just a few seconds later. It is suggested, therefore, that specimens should be mounted side by side for easy comparison. It is possible to obtain very large polarisers (200mm x 200mm or larger), but smaller ones are obviously cheaper and easier to obtain, and, if these are used, a double side-by-side polariscope is recommended.

Since demonstrations will be given to fairly large groups, it is important to keep the polariser and analyser as close together as possible, to provide a wide field of view.

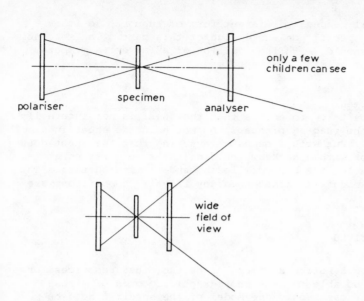

only a few
children can see

polariser   specimen   analyser

wide
field of
view

However, if the polariser and analyser are close together, it is
very difficult to position the specimen. It is therefore suggested
that the analyser and the straining frame should be easily removable
from the polariscope.

Construction of a straining frame

The straining frame must provide a wide range of fixing positions,
and for this reason Meccano is very suitable.

load

Each specimen will demand a different form of support, so it is impossible to be specific on the design of this part. The Meccano framework shown should, with the addition of a few extra members, provide a means of holding most specimens.

Shaping the specimen

Great care must be taken to ensure that the sheet is not internally stressed during the shaping process. Do not hold the sheet in a vice at any time. Cut with a bandsaw (ensuring that the sheet does not become hot) or with a hacksaw, holding the sheet flat on a bench by hand. Holes are best drilled by end-milling cutters. The specimen must be made with great accuracy if valid comparisons are to be made.

POSSIBLE ALTERNATIVES

Schools possessing a Polaroid camera or having other resources for photography will be able to make photographic records of stress patterns. In this case, only one model of the specimen need be made, and only one polariser/analyser pair will be required.

Literature, obtainable from CIBA (UK) Ltd, Duxford, Cambs, describes the production of models in Araldite resin which is highly sensitive to small changes in stress. Moreover, the stress pattern can be 'preserved' by baking the model together with the loading frame. On cooling, the model can be viewed without the need to reload.

Suppliers of equipment and further information

Welwyn Electric, Teddington, Middlesex
Polarisers (UK) Ltd, Lincoln Road, Cressex Estate, High Wycombe, Bucks.

For further guidance on photoelastic techniques see 'Photoelasticity for Schools and Colleges' published by NCST, Trent Polytechnic, Nottingham.

Appendix 2

STRAIN-GAUGES

The use of strain-gauges on model structures

The resistance strain-gauge is a useful device for determining the magnitude and the kind of force (compressive or tensile) present in structural members. A high-gain amplifier is required to amplify the effect of the small changes which take place in the resistance of a strain-gauge attached to a member in tension, compression, or bending.

It is not practicable to use strain-gauges on Meccano strip for two reasons:

a) Meccano strip is easily bent, and may be appreciably so even when new;

b) the presence of holes in the material results in a complex force distribution when the material is loaded.

For these reasons, if it is desired to obtain the relative sizes of the forces in members or, more simply, to determine whether or not a member is in tension or compression, the relevant Meccano member is removed and replaced by a length of strip or angle Perspex (3mm in thickness) to which a suitable strain-gauge has been attached. It is not necessary to have Perspex replicas of every size of Meccano angle and strip. Provided that no holes are present within about 25mm either side of the strain-gauge, a long strip can be made and used to replace any length of Meccano. In most cases the resulting projection of Perspex from the model will not invalidate the test.

- 3mm thick Perspex strip approx Meccano width
- Sellotape
- strain gauge
- soldered joints
- insulated leads
- 4mm plugs

4 mm plugs

strain-gauge
cemented in position

Sellotape for protection

two strips of Perspex
cemented together to
produce angle

projection

structure
under test

It is recommended that, if a test is to be made to determine whether
a member is in tension or compression, angle material made from
Perspex is used, since this will not bend under compression. When
tests are made to find the relative size of forces in members, it
must be remembered that only members of the same section can be
compared.

Fixing strain-gauges
Clean the Perspex with a degreasing agent which will not attack the
material e.g. methylated spirit. Alternatively, use very fine glass
paper or emery cloth over an area slightly larger than the gauge.
Apply a thin layer of quick-drying adhesive (type CH - supplied by
Electro Mechanisms Ltd) to the back of the gauge, place the gauge
in position on the Perspex, cover with a small piece of polyethylene

sheet, and press in place between the fingers for about one minute. Remove the polyethylene sheet and leave to set fully for about thirty minutes.

Cut the gauge leads, leaving about 6mm of free lead, and carefully solder on to each an extension lead of insulated wire about 500mm long. Secure the extension leads to the Perspex and protect the gauge by wrapping Sellotape tightly round the member. Fit 4mm plugs on the extension lead.

RESISTANCE CHANGES IN STRAIN-GAUGES

If the gauge is fitted as shown, the following changes in resistance occur when the member is in tension, compression or bending.

a) Member in tension - resistance increases.

b) Member in compression - resistance decreases.

c) Member in bending - top in tension, resistance increases.

d) Member in bending - top in compression, resistance decreases.

From these diagrams it is apparent why a single Perspex strip should not be used to determine whether a member is in tension or compression. If the member bends when in compression it could do so in either direction, thus it is possible to obtain an increase in resistance (diagram d)) suggesting that the member is in tension.

STRAIN-GAUGE AMPLIFIER

A high-gain d.c. amplifier free from appreciable 'drift' is a complex and expensive item, but in recent years schools have con-structed low-cost instruments based on readily available (integrated circuit) operational amplifiers.

For guidance on the construction of a strain-gauge bridge using an operational amplifier, refer to Op-amp Applications, published by NCST, Trent Polytechnic, Nottingham.

Appendix 3

CAPACITORS

The pupils will have used a capacitor in conjunction with a relay in the Electrical-switching assignments in order to produce a 'delay device'. The simple theory of capacitors is probably best covered by simple experiments, working in groups, and by teacher demonstrations. The following procedure should be adopted.

1 Discuss the effects when using the delay circuit in the vehicle. The idea of a capacitor acting as a short-term battery or reservoir may well be put forward. Emphasise this 'delay' function, since the capacitor is included as one of the three main devices which can be used in conjunction with logic arrangements which may come later.

These arrangements are:

    the clock (oscillator),
    the delay (monostable), and
    the flip-flop (bistable).

2 Each group is asked to connect a capacitor (about $5000\mu F$) across the terminals of a 12V battery. The supply is removed and the capacitor terminals are then shorted out. Discuss the implications of a spark appearing. The storing of an electrical charge should be emphasised, and it may be wise at this stage to again discuss the difference between 'charge' and 'current'.

3 'What determines the amount of charge stored?'
The pupils should be encouraged to try different voltages and different values of capacitor (not capacitors in parallel to increase the value at this stage). Since the size of spark gives an indication of the quantity of charge stored, they should come to the conclusion that:

a) the larger the voltage used, the greater the charge stored; and
b) the larger the value of the capacitor, the greater the charge stored.

With able pupils we could suggest:

$$Q \alpha C$$
$$Q \alpha V$$
$$\therefore Q \alpha CV$$

The units of capacitance - the farad (F), microfarad (μF), and picofarad ($\mu \mu F$ or pF) - should be explained. The main point to be made is that the larger the number of microfarads, the larger the storage capacity of the capacitor.

4   Pupils should then be encouraged to use capacitors in parallel,
    using a 12V d.c. supply. It will be seen that the capacitance
    increases if two or more capacitors are connected in parallel.
    Hence two 5000μF capacitors in parallel produce a total capaci-
    tance of 10 000μF, three 5000μF capacitors in parallel give
    15 000μF, and so on.

5   The effect of capacitors in series could be investigated, but
    the application of this arrangement in project work is likely
    to be very limited during the course.

6   Teachers may wish to discharge a capacitor through an ammeter to
    show current flow, to reinforce the spark demonstration. Capa-
    citors of about 5000μF charged up using a 12V d.c. supply produce
    adequate deflections on a 0-1 A ammeter. It should be appreci-
    ated, however, that the inertia of the moving parts of the
    ammeter may result in very low values of current being indicated.

7   The delay function of a capacitor is an important item in the
    course and should, therefore, be treated quite fully. If a
    capacitor is charged from a battery, then removed from the supply
    and discharged by placing a piece of wire across the capacitor
    leads, it can be seen that the charge and discharge are virtually
    instantaneous. However, if the charge or discharge operation is
    carried out with a resistance in series with the capacitor (e.g.
    a resistor or a relay coil) the charge and discharge times are
    much slower. This effect should be shown using resistors, since
    the pupils will have noticed the effect using a relay. We must
    show that the resistance of the relay coil is related to the
    delay time produced. The following experiments are suggested:

    a) Connect a 12V, 2.2W bulb across a 12V supply. Remove one
       lead from the supply and note how rapidly the bulb is extin-
       guished. Charge a 5000μF capacitor from a 12V supply (d.c.).
       Discharge it through the same bulb and note the slight delay
       before the bulb finally goes out.

    b) Charge a 5000μF capacitor from a 12V d.c. supply. Discharge
       the capacitor through a robust moving-coil ammeter (0-1A).
       Note the rapid discharge.

       Note: A large instantaneous current will flow initially, and
       this could damage a fragile meter.

Place a resistor of about a 2000 ohms in series with a 0-10mA
meter (the 0-10mA range on an Avometer model 7 is suitable).
Note the slow charge and discharge rates. Draw graphs of
charging current plotted against time and discharging current
against time, with the aid of a stopwatch.

From graphs such as these, we can calculate the delay time
which will be obtained with a 5000μF capacitor in parallel
with a relay of coil resistance 2000 ohm, when the minimum
holding current of the relay is known.

Discuss the results of these experiments and indicate how the
delay time for a capacitor discharging through a relay is mainly
dependent upon the resistance of the relay coil. To emphasise
this fact, it is recommended that a number of relays, with
different coil resistances, be tested and the delay times found.

8 Show a number of different types of capacitor, relating physical
size and type to capacitance. The importance of correct polarity
when using electrolytic types could be discussed and a comparison
made with other types.

Appendix 4

ASSESSMENT OF PUPILS TAKING CONTROL TECHNOLOGY

WRITTEN PAPERS

To produce a written examination consistent with the course aims, the papers for the second and third years are divided into clearly defined sections.

SECTION A Short questions on facts and principles included in basic course assignments (cheap recall). These may or may not be multiple choice.

SECTION B Longer questions on basic course material (expensive recall).

SECTION C Fault finding

SECTION D Analysis of structures, systems, circuits etc. Pupils are expected to give precise descriptions and explanations.

SECTION E Synthesis - a design problem. This is similar in principle to the kind of specification given for a project.

The information given above is directly relevant to teachers having the same aims as those which were taken into account during the development of the course. Those teachers having very different aims may find it useful for guidance

PRACTICAL TEST

A number of simple experiments (ideally, equal to the number of pupils in the group) are set up.

Pupils have 5 minutes at each experiment, in which time the practical work and the recording of observations, results, and calculations, if necessary, must be completed on the answer paper.

In this way the pupil's ability to handle and use equipment, to translate actual circuits into circuit diagrams, to record observations, and to interpret results, is assessed.

A specimen practical examination paper is given overleaf.

SPECIMEN EXAMINATION PAPER: PRACTICAL EXAMINATION

You are allowed _five minutes_ at each set of equipment. When you have finished, leave each piece of equipment exactly as you found it.

Answers alone are insufficient. Ensure that you briefly, but clearly, indicate how you arrived at each answer, since the assessment of your performance is based upon your written account.

1 Plot a graph of ammeter reading, on the 0-100 scale, against time for the discharging capacitor. To charge the capacitor, depress the switch for about 5 seconds. On releasing the switch, the capacitor discharges through the resistor in the box and the ammeter. Take scale readings every 10 seconds for a total time of one minute.

2 Estimate the pressure in N/mm^2 being supplied to the 24mm diameter double-acting pneumatic cylinder.
Show all calculations.

3 Make a clear circuit diagram of this relay oscillator.

4 What is the speed of the motor armature?

5 Plot a graph to show how the strain-gauge meter reading varies with the load, for loads of 0.1 to 0.7 kg in steps of 0.1 kg. What relationship does the graph suggest?

6 Identify the type of gear system used in the box and suggest the number of teeth on each gear.

7 The box contains two diodes. Between which sockets are the diodes connected? To which sockets are the diode anodes and cathodes connected?

8

A	B	C	Result

For all positions of the switches, fill in the table to indicate when the lamp illuminates or fails to illuminate (i.e. result 1 or 0).

9 Switch on the supply and record the voltage across the relay coil and the current flowing in it. From the results, calculate the relay coil resistance.

10 Using the ohmmeter, identify which of the three transistors - A, B, and C - are pnp and which are npn.

11 Under the load shown, state whether the members A, B, and C are in tension, compression, or bending?

12 Draw an electrical equivalent of the pneumatic circuit.

13 Using the colour code provided, identify the value and tolerance of each of the four resistors. If any of them are of the high-stability type, indicate this.

14 Using the relay delay circuit, estimate the value of the capacitor C by comparing its effect with that of the 2000μF capacitor. Apart from removing and fitting the capacitors, make no changes to the arrangement.

15 Using the ohmmeter only, identify the electronic components in box A and box B.

16 The current gain of a transistor is given by:

$$\text{current gain } (h_{FE}) = \frac{\text{collector current}}{\text{base current}}$$

Calculate the gain of the transistor in the arrangement.

MARKING OF WRITTEN QUESTIONS

Since the questions usually require a number of part-answers, it is recommended that a detailed marking scheme is made for each question, and a mark awarded for each correct statement. A marking scheme for question D2 in the specimen examination paper which follows could be:

Sequence of Events

1 Both oscillators oscillate continuously (1 mark). RL5 energised (1).

2 Switch A depressed, RL7 energises (1). U1 energises (1). L1 on (1).

3 Switch A released, RL7 de-energises (1). U1 de-energises (1). U1,1 to position 2 (1). RL6 energises (1). L2 on (1).

4 Via slow oscillator, U1 steps slowly (1). L3, 4, 5, 6, 7, and 8 illuminate in turn (1).

5 When L8 illuminates, RL6 de-energises (1). (RL5 de-energised) fast oscillator steps U1 (1). L9, 10, 11, and 12 illuminate in turn (1).

6 When L1 illuminates, RL5 energises (1). Sequence stops (1).
TOTAL 17 Marks

The total mark for the paper can be converted to a percentage mark by graphical methods:

EXAMINATION PAPER

<u>Note</u>: The content of the examination papers written at a particular school will vary from year to year and will, to some extent, reflect the topic emphasis in a given group. Teachers should not feel obliged to include all the techniques reflected in these specimen questions. For instance, uniselectors had been used frequently in a major group project in this school, and therefore a section D question was included to cover this topic in the examination.

Similarly, teachers should not conclude that a full coverage of pneumatic control is essential to thè course, especially during the development phase. However, a knowledge of pneumatic equipment and control is very desirable in the long term.

Specimen Paper   CONTROL TECHNOLOGY

                    5th FORM MOCK CSE EXAMINATION   Time 2½ hours

Section A - Answer ALL questions

Indicate the answer you think is the correct one by writing the appropriate letter in the space provided.

1   If, for the crane shown above, the load is 4000 kg and the counter-weight is 10 000 kg, the distance 'd' for balance is

              A   2.5m
              B   5.0m
              C   8.0m
              D   20.0m
              E   50.0m

. . . .

2 The diagram shows a lorry trailer carrying a load W   The
action of the load produces

       A compressive forces at both X and Y
       B compressive force at X and tensile forces at Y
       C tensile forces at both X and Y
       D tensile forces at X and compressive forces at Y
       E none of these

X = top surface
Y = bottom surface

3 In a lifting device, a 50 tooth gear is driven by a worm gear.
If an effort of 1000 ℕ just raises a load of 16 000 N, the
efficiency of the system is

       A 2%
       B 10%
       C 16%
       D 32%
       E 50%

4

disc A

rubber tyre B
50 mm diameter
360 rev/min

Disc A is rotated about point O by rubber tyre B. For A to
rotate at 45 rev/min, the distance from B to point O must be

    A   80mm
    B   90mm
    C   200mm
    D   400mm
    E   720mm

....

5

Six identical 1.5v cells are connected as shown. The voltage
measured between A and B is

    A   0V
    B   3.0V
    C   4.5V
    D   6.0V
    E   9.0V

....

6   A vehicle moves at 30mm/s. If the driving wheels, driven
directly by the motor, have a circumference of 50mm, the speed
of the motor is

    A   5rev/min
    B   6rev/min
    C   30rev/min
    D 150rev/min
    E 360rev/min

....

7   To make a d.c. electric motor change from a clockwise to an
anticlockwise rotation the switch required would be a

    A   single-pole on-off
    B   double-pole on-off
    C   single-pole change-over
    D   double-pole change-over
    E   any of these

....

8   Relays are frequently employed in electrical circuitry for all
of the following <u>except</u>

A   to enable large currents to be switched by small
    currents
B   to act as a delay
C   to act as an inverter
D   to enable small currents to be switched by large
    currents
E   to act as a memory

....

9   A capacitor of value 1000μF keeps a relay energised for 10
    seconds. To produce a delay of approximately 30 seconds,
    which of the following could be used?

A   three 1000μF capacitors connected in parallel
B   three 1000μF capacitors connected in series
C   a 2000μF capacitor in series with a 1000 F
D   two 3000μF capacitors connected in parallel
E   two 3000μF capacitors connected in series

....

10 A light-dependent resistor (photocell) is used in electrical
    and electronic circuits for all the following reasons except

A   it acts as a switch for small currents
B   it can be used as a variable resistor
C   it may be used to compare amounts of light incident
    upon it
D   it is not easily damaged by large currents
E   its resistance changes can be from a few ohms to
    many thousands of ohms

....

11 When using a 20mm dia. pneumatic cylinder, the approximate air
    pressure to produce a force of 30N is

A   0.2N/mm^2
B   0.5N/mm^2
C   2.0N/mm^2
D   5.0N/mm^2
E   10.0N/mm^2

....

12 If the voltage to an electrical solenoid is doubled, the force
    produced on the armature is

A   reduced by a factor of 2
B   doubled
C   more than doubled
D   increased but does not double
E   unchanged

....

13 All the following mechanisms produce continuous reciprocating linear motion from continuous rotary motion <u>except</u> the

    A cam and follower
    B crank and slider
    C eccentric
    D peg and slot
    E rack and pinion

....

14 The speed of movement of the piston of a double-acting pneumatic cylinder is usually controlled by means of

    A an exhaust restrictor fitted directly to the cylinder
    B an exhaust restrictor fitted to an appropriate valve
    C a diaphragm valve fitted to the cylinder
    D a reservoir fitted between the cylinder and its control valve
    E a reduction of pressure of the primary air supply

....

15

When valve Z in the arrangement above is operated, and left in the operated position, the cylinder piston rod extends after a delay time. All of the following increase the delay time <u>except</u>

    A increasing the volume of X
    B further restricting the flow through Y
    C increasing the volume of X and further restricting the flow through Y
    D reducing the supply pressure
    E increasing the flow through Y

....

16 When three resistors of the same value are connected in parallel, the resulting effective resistance is 24 ohms. The value of each resistor is

    A   3 ohm
    B   8 ohm
    C   24 ohm
    D   36 ohm
    E   72 ohm

....

17 A coil of 30 ohm resistance is connected across a 12V supply. The most suitable fuse to protect the circuit is

    A 500mA
    B 2.5A
    C 3.0A
    D 10.0A
    E 30.0A

....

18 A resistor has a value of 50 ohm and a 0.5 watt power rating. The greatest continuous current it is designed to carry is

    A 10mA
    B 20mA
    C 40mA
    D 100mA
    E 500mA

....

19 A half-wave rectifier circuit contains a transformer and

    A one diode
    B two diodes
    C three diodes
    D four diodes
    E more than four diodes

....

20 An npn transistor can pass an appreciable collector-emitter current if

    A the base is more positive than the emitter
    B the base is left disconnected
    C the collector is more negative than the base and emitter
    D the base is more negative than the emitter
    E the emitter is disconnected

....

Section B - Answer ALL questions   Use the A4 paper provided

1 Draw a circuit diagram of an arrangement which will enable a motor to start when an on-off switch is closed. The motor should switch off several seconds after the switch is opened. Explain the operation of your circuit.

2 By means of a short description and a circuit diagram, show how you would use a transistor arrangement to make a warning lamp illuminate when a beam of light to a photocell is broken.

3 Draw a pneumatic circuit which would cause the piston of a double-acting cylinder to oscillate continuously.

Section C - Answer ALL questions

There is one fault in each of the following systems. In each case indicate the fault on the A4 paper provided. (In some cases a corrected diagram may be necessary.)

4

When switch A in this circuit is momentarily depressed, the motor is intended to run and to continue running for several seconds, after which it should stop automatically. There is one incorrect connection. Redraw the circuit in order that it will function correctly, indicating clearly the original error.

5

Answer <u>both</u> questions on the A4 paper provided.

1

Cylinder X, fixed to plate K, clamps the strip of metal to platform L, which is also attached to part K.

Cylinder Y moves cylinder X and parts K and L together as a unit, as indicated by the arrow. The movement of this unit is limited by the mechanical stop which incorporates valve G.

What will happen when an impulse is applied at valve A? Fully explain the operation of the circuit.

Trace and describe the sequence of events in the circuit when
an impulse is applied by the manual push button A.

All relay contacts are shown adjacent to their respective coils,
Ul is a uniselector coil. Ul,1 and Ul,2 are the uniselector
switch banks. Separate power supplies are shown to preserve
clarity. The earth symbol (⏚) represents a common negative
terminal to all supplies.

Section E

Design a traffic-light control system for a crossroads which allows N-S traffic to flow for 20 seconds and E-W traffic for 30 seconds. The system should also take into account:

a) If E-W traffic is heavy, the time should be extended to 40 seconds.

b) If no N-S traffic is waiting to cross the junction, then E-W traffic should continue to flow until waiting vehicles occur N-S.

METHOD OF ASSESSMENT

An example of a proposed method of assessment, submitted by a school to an examining board.

Control Technology

CSE MODE III

Continuous Assessment

Marks to be awarded for the following:

1   Examinations a) Written
                 b) Practical

2   Projects   a) 4th year main project
                b) 5th year major project

3   Files - course work

The marks will be awarded over the two years in the following manner:

4th year (2nd year of course)	40%
5th year (3rd year of course)	50%

There will be a margin of 10% which may be allotted to candidates following a viva with the moderator.

Marks are also awarded for the total three years course and practical work and assimilation of control techniques.

NB   Usual grading method used.

4th year	40%
Written examination	15%
Practical examination	10%
Course work	5%
Main project	10%

<u>5th year</u>   50%
Written examination	20%
Practical examination	10%
Course work	5%
Major project	15%

<u>Breakdown</u>
Written examinations	35%
Practical examinations	20%
Course work	10%
Projects	25%
Viva	<u>10%</u>
	100%

Editorial Note:

It must be stressed that this example is given to provide general guidance only, and should not be regarded as setting a rigid pattern for an acceptable proposal.

Appendix 5

COURSE EQUIPMENT

Background

Throughout the development of the CONTROL TECHNOLOGY Course it was recognised that much of the work to be carried out by the pupils, and the teaching methods to be adopted, should be based, primarily, on the use of a range of purpose-built equipment. In devising the apparatus which would effectively complement the pupils' texts, careful consideration was given to factors such as availability, costs, appearance, practicality and durability.

A policy of continuous development and modification of the basic equipment was adopted during the period of trials, and later, thus reflecting the day-to-day experience in the schools. Not only was the equipment to be of central importance for the boy or girl working sequentially through the programme of assignments and investigations, but it was to be used extensively in project work at various stages in the course.

With all of these aspects in mind, and conscious of the various pressures on the schools, negotiations have taken place with a number of manufacturers which have resulted in substantial savings to those schools placing orders for complete kits. In addition, agreement has been reached regarding simplified ordering procedures, thereby avoiding the frustrating use of extensive and complicated parts lists.

Up-to-date information on the provision of the complete equipment for the course is available from:

> The National Centre for School Technology,
> Trent Polytechnic,
> Burton Street,
> Nottingham.